30 Questions

ABOUT THE

Japanese Art

OF THE

Kimono

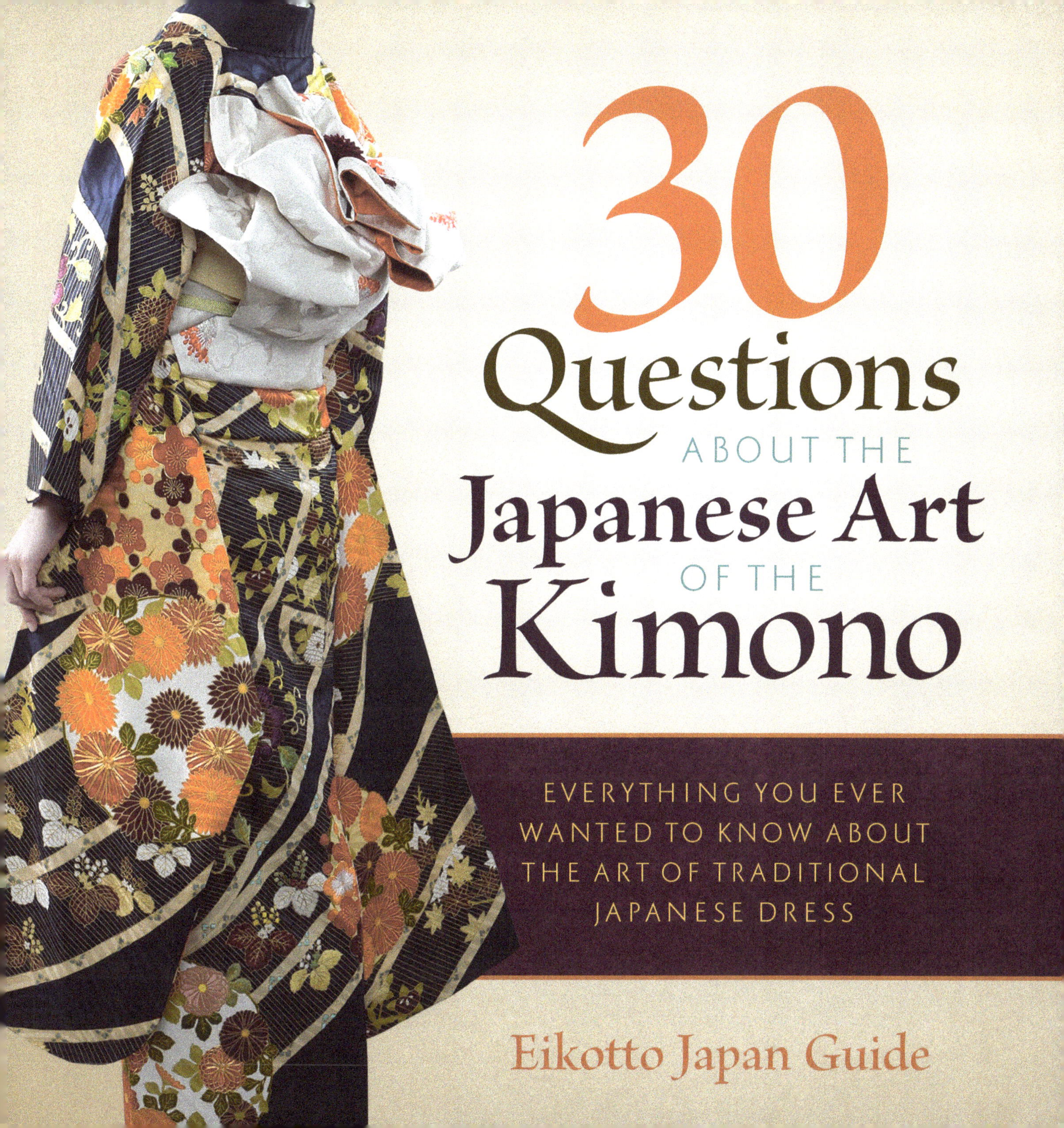

30 Questions

ABOUT THE

Japanese Art

OF THE

Kimono

EVERYTHING YOU EVER
WANTED TO KNOW ABOUT
THE ART OF TRADITIONAL
JAPANESE DRESS

Eikotto Japan Guide

Thirty Questions About the Japanese Art of the Kimono: Everything You Ever Wanted to Know about the Art of Traditional Japanese Dress

For information about this title or to order other books and/or electronic media, contact the publisher:

Eikotto Japan Guide
Eiko Ito
https://eikottojapanguide.com
info@eikottojapanguide.com

Japan E-book Technology Dissemination Association (JETDA)
1-11-4-1000 Umeda, Kita-ku, Osaka 5300001

ISBNs:
978-4-910472-46-1 (print)
978-4-910472-47-8 (eBook)

Printed in the United States of America

Cover and Interior design: 1106 Design

Illustrations by an Illustrator, Tomoko Kubotani, *http://tomokokubotani.blog.fc2.com/*

First edition 27 July 2021

For all the guests I have guided and I will see in the future.

ACKNOWLEDGMENTS

I want to express my sincere gratitude to an illustrator, Tomoko Kubotani, who drew lovely illustrations for this book.

I am also incredibly grateful to Misuzu and Issaku, who made Japanese poems and took pictures for this book, a historical kimono shop owner, Mr. Tadaaki Yamazaki, who gave me precious advice about kimono, and Ms. Andrea Costa, who advised me about current English expressions for this book.

Finally, thanks are due to Ms. Michele Defilippo and Ms. Ronda Rawlins from 1106 Design, who advised me on publishing this book.

As a tour guide for more than ten years, I have hosted more than a thousand overseas guests to Japan. I have noticed that certain questions come up again and again. I thought it would be helpful to have a book that answers the most common questions about the ancient Japanese art of the kimono.

Japanese people have sensitive feelings toward nature.

In the West, people tend to dress according to time, place, and occasion. In contrast, Japanese kimonos are worn according to season, place, and occasion. Kimono standards of dress reflect even slight seasonal changes with colors and patterns. Nature is the principal model for kimono color coordination.

Additionally, formal occasions require that a kimono utilize "auspicious"—happy and ceremonial—patterns and colors. If you come to Japan, you might have a chance to see a wedding-ceremony procession at a shrine. It is fun to observe the attendants' kimonos when you have some understanding of their meanings. One interesting thing that a kimono can tell you is the attendant's background. For example, you can tell who the mothers of the bride and groom are just by looking at their kimonos.

It is easier to understand the Japanese art of the kimono by knowing the two main groups—the *modern* kimono and the *traditional* kimono. In my opinion, if you learn traditional kimonos, you can enjoy modern kimonos much more because some of the contemporary kimonos use conventional handicraft techniques. They often have messages from the styles, patterns, and colors.

When visiting popular tourist spots such as Asakusa (see Chapter 1), you may see many people dressed in kimonos. Many of these kimonos are examples of the modern casual kimono. It is easy to find shops that provide kimono-wearing experiences to tourists, which are a lovely chance to try this type of Japanese kimono.

However, if you take the time to learn about the traditional kimono, you will understand the real attraction of the kimono as an *art*. Traditional kimonos utilize sophisticated Japanese handicraft techniques that have developed through centuries of history.

In Chapter 1, I will introduce casual kimonos for everyone. From Chapter 2 to Chapter 8, I will mainly explain traditional kimonos according to the historical classification. In Chapter 9, I will introduce recommended shops so that anyone can enjoy kimonos.

I hope you appreciate the profound attraction of Japanese kimonos.

CONTENTS

Like the Japanese kimono, Western clothing has its own set of "dress codes" and "ranks."

On many occasions, Western clothing is chosen according to some dress code. In formal situations, a dress code is typically set by the host and stated in the invitation letter. It is considered inappropriate to wear something more or less formal than what is designated by the host, or otherwise different from the attire worn by other attendees.

To make the dress codes and ranks of the Japanese kimono easier to understand, I used typical classifications of Western attire as a comparison. To clarify the classification of Western clothes that I used in this book, examples are stated in the table of the next page for reference.

CLASSIFICATION	DESCRIPTION AND EXAMPLES
Formal attire	*Clothing that is worn when a dress code is set as described below.* **Men:** Full formal dress **Example:** Morning coat, white tie (tailcoat), black tie (tuxedo) **Women:** Full formal dress **Example:** Afternoon dress, evening dress **Situations:** National ceremonies, international events, etc.
Semiformal attire	*Clothing that is worn when a dress code is set as described below.* **Men:** Semiformal dress **Example:** Director's suit, black suit, fancy tuxedo **Women:** Semiformal dress **Example:** Dinner dress, cocktail dress **Situations:** International events, commonly held ceremonies, etc.
Informal attire	*Clothing that is worn when a dress code is not set.* **Men:** Suit style (more formal than casual attire but has no strict restrictions) **Example:** Dark suit **Women:** Suit style or smart casual style with a level of formality higher than casual attire **Situations:** Corporate commemorative events and receptions, commonly held events and parties, etc.
Casual attire	*Clothing that is normally worn on a day-to-day basis.* **Men and Women:** Western casual clothing, including T-shirt, jeans.

Reference: *Fundamentals of the Modern Protocols, published by The Japan Education Centre for the Hotel Industry, 2017, Chapter 4: Formal attire and decorations, pp. 148–165*

CHAPTER 1

Casual Kimonos

1) *Yukata*: Traditional casual cotton kimonos

QUESTION 1

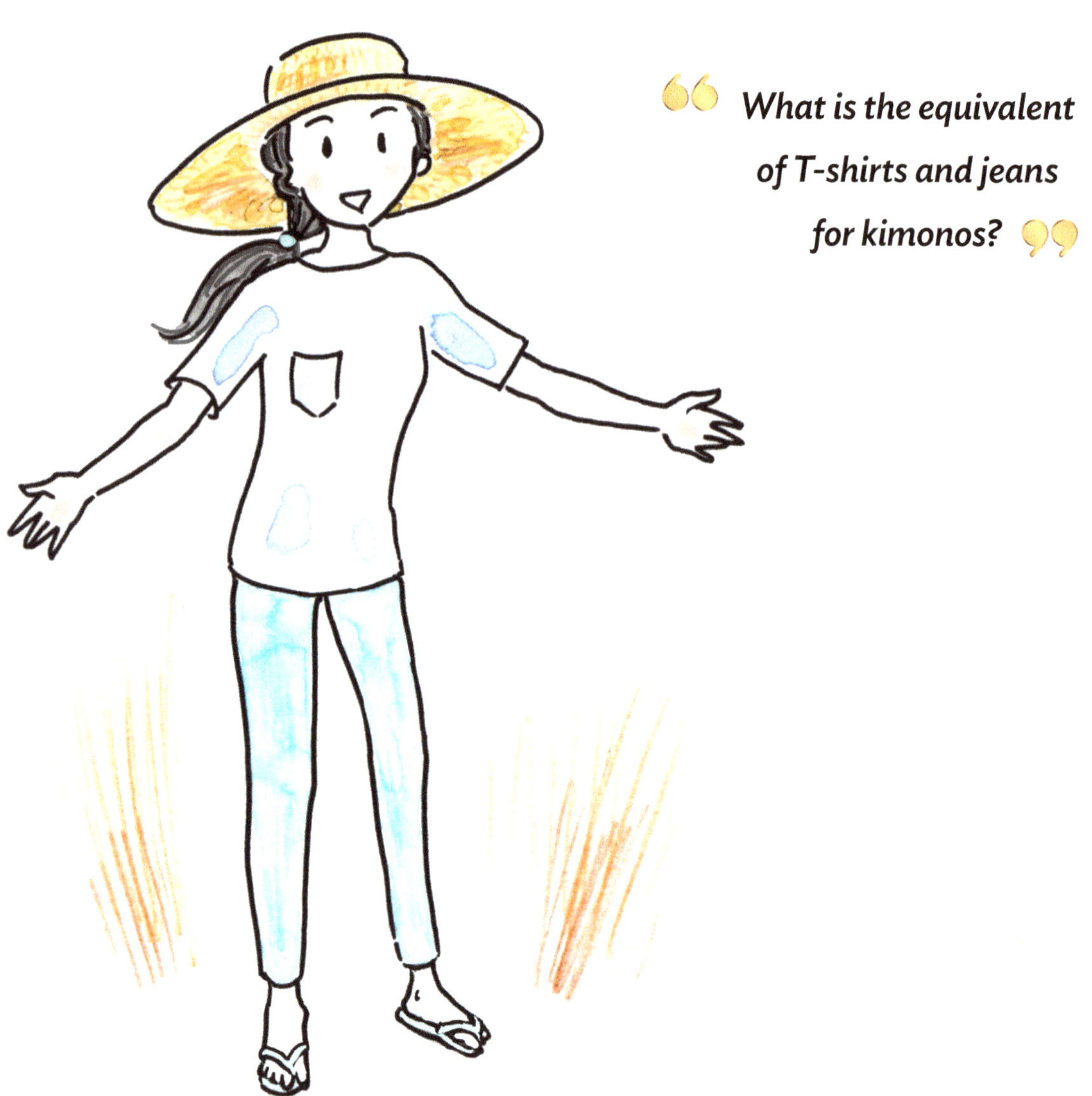

*What is the equivalent
of T-shirts and jeans
for kimonos?*

ANSWER 1

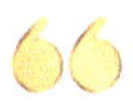 ***Yukata** are single-collar kimonos made of cotton. They are worn in casual situations, similar to casual T-shirts, sweatshirts, tracksuits, or jeans. They belong to the traditional kimono group.* 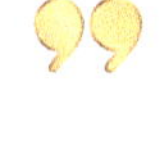

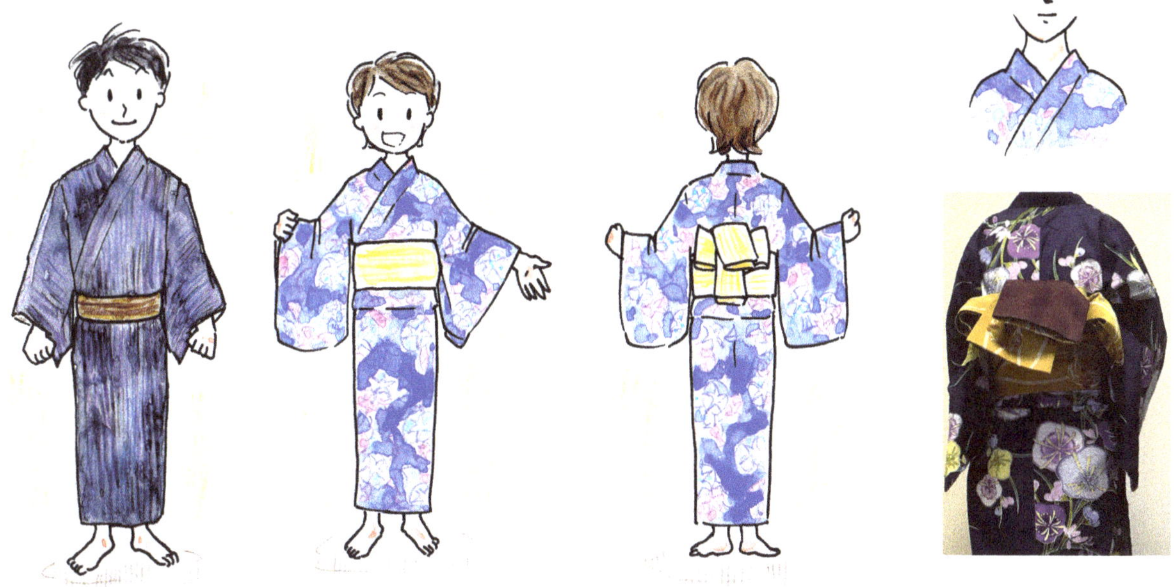

Because people usually wear this type of kimono during summertime, the patterns are typically suitable for summer.

Yukata initially started as a bathrobe around the 10th century in Japan. This is why they belong to the traditional kimono group, even though they are also regarded as casual kimonos.

Yukata are always made of **cotton**. They are very popular as a souvenir for overseas tourists because of their ease of care. People can enjoy *yukata* in a variety of colors and patterns.

QUESTION 2

" *What is the equivalent to nightwear or loungewear for kimonos at Japanese-style inns?* "

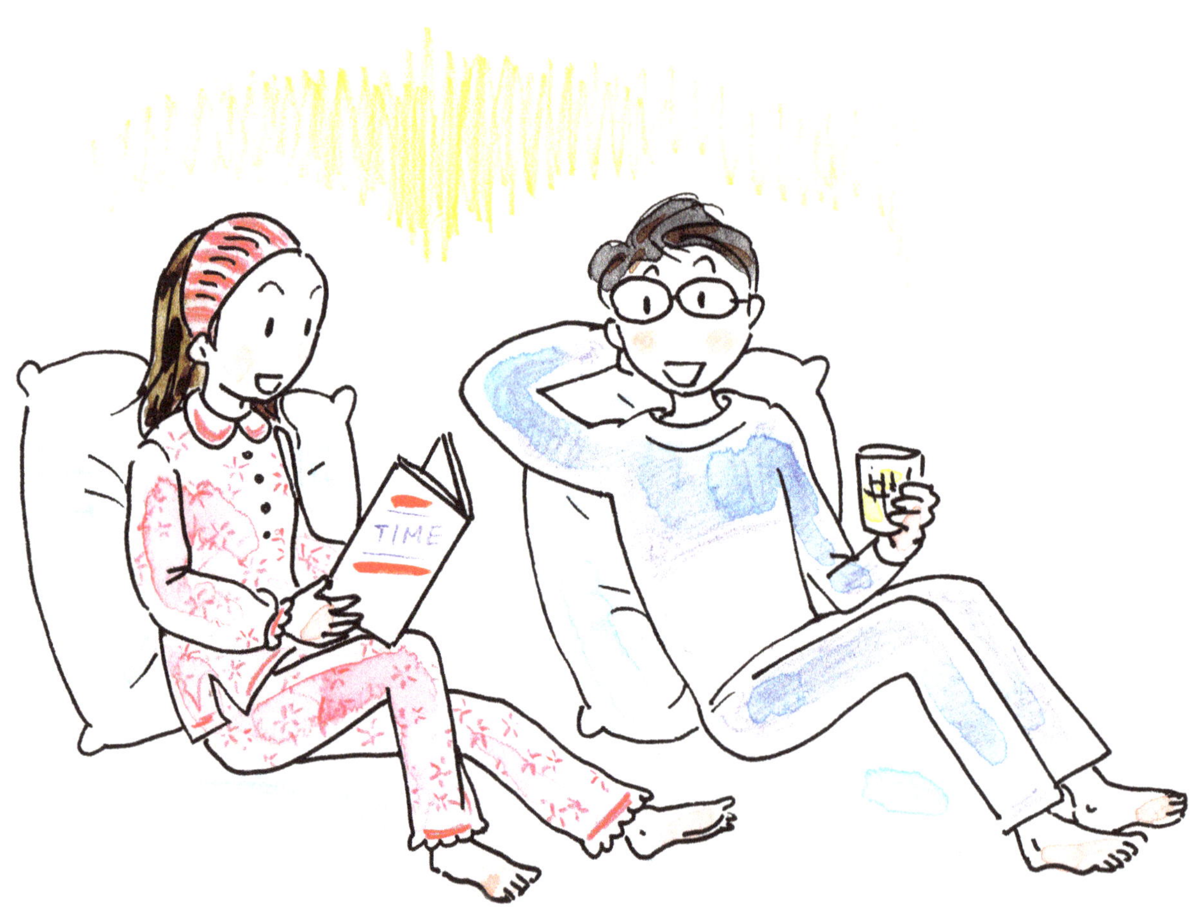

ANSWER 2

*Japanese-style inns often provide guests with a type of **yukata** to use as nightwear or loungewear. These yukata are much simpler than **yukata** for outside wear but are also made of cotton. People can relax in **yukata** comfortably at Japanese-style inns—just as they do at home.*

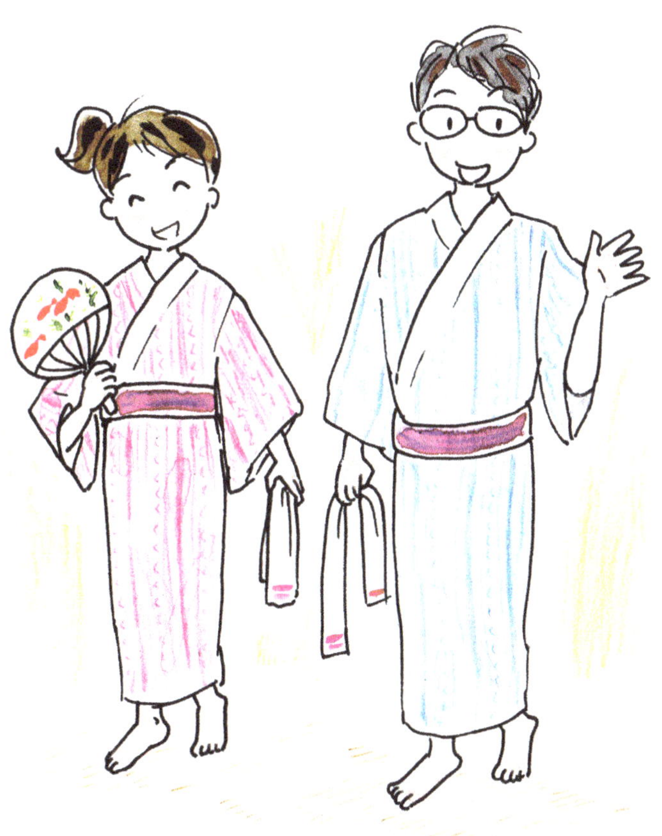

2) Modern casual kimonos

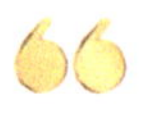

*What is the kimono equivalent
to Western casual clothing?*

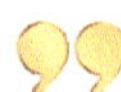

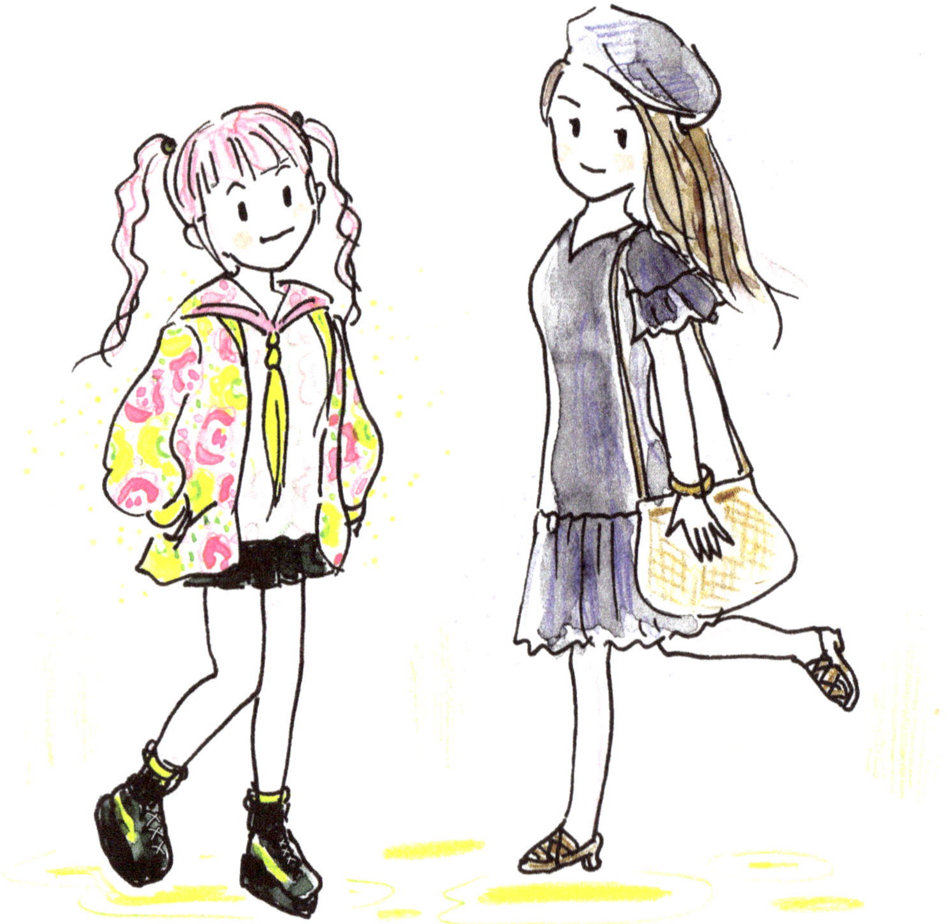

ANSWER 3

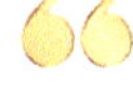 *Modern casual kimonos.*

They are most commonly worn by tourists. 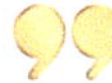

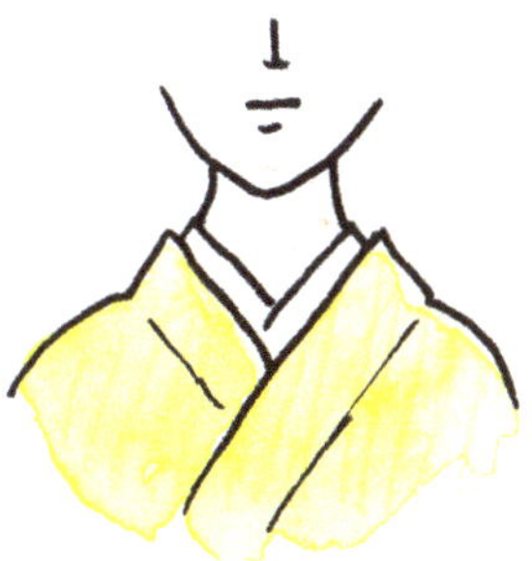

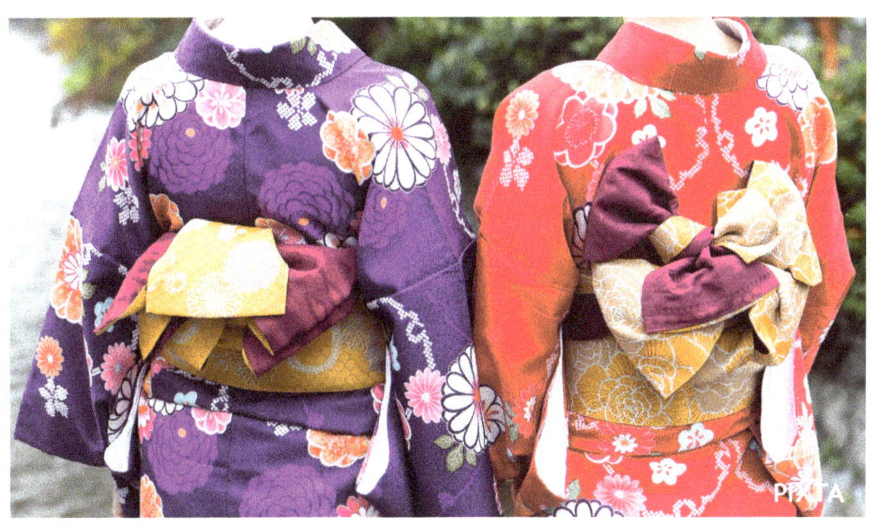

Modern casual kimonos look similar to *yukata*. The significant differences between them are the materials and collars. Modern casual kimonos are often made of colorful **polyester** and have **double-layered collars**.

Asakusa
A popular spot in Tokyo to buy yukata and to experience modern casual kimonos

For those who would like to experience the modern casual kimono, Asakusa is the most recommended spot in Tokyo.

In this area, there are many tourists dressed in kimonos. It is an exciting experience to drop by a kimono-experience shop, put on a modern casual kimono, and enjoy walking around this historical spot for a day. After enjoying the kimono, just return to the shop and change clothes. It is easy to find this kind of shop in Asakusa.

This area also has many shops that sell the traditional cotton kimonos called *yukata*. Past the main gate of Sensoji temple, there is one of the oldest shopping streets in Tokyo, Nakamise Street.

*There are also some shops which provide traditional kimono experiences.

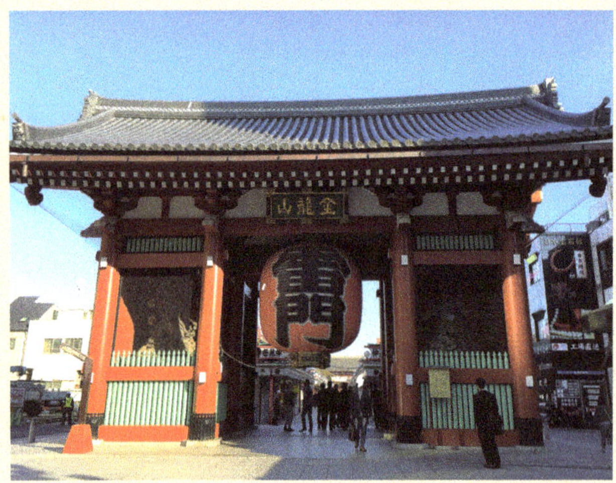
Sensoji Temple

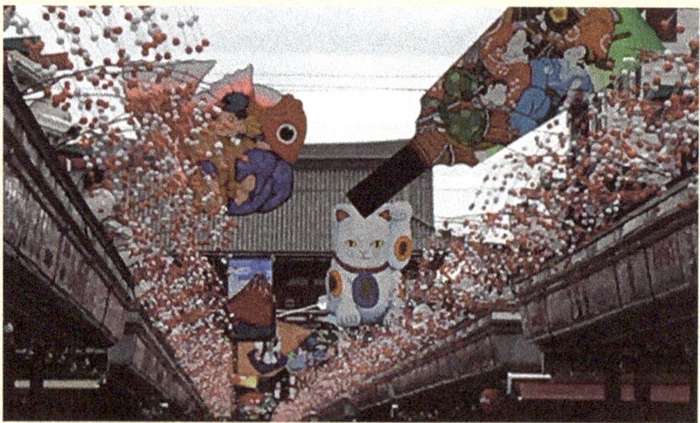
New Year Decorations at Nakamise Street

Access:

Subway Ginza Line Asakusa Station (G19)
Subway Toei Asakusa Line Asakusa Station (A18)
Tobu Isesaki Line Asakusa Station (TS01)

Traditional Kimonos for Special Occasions

1) Wedding kimonos

QUESTION 4

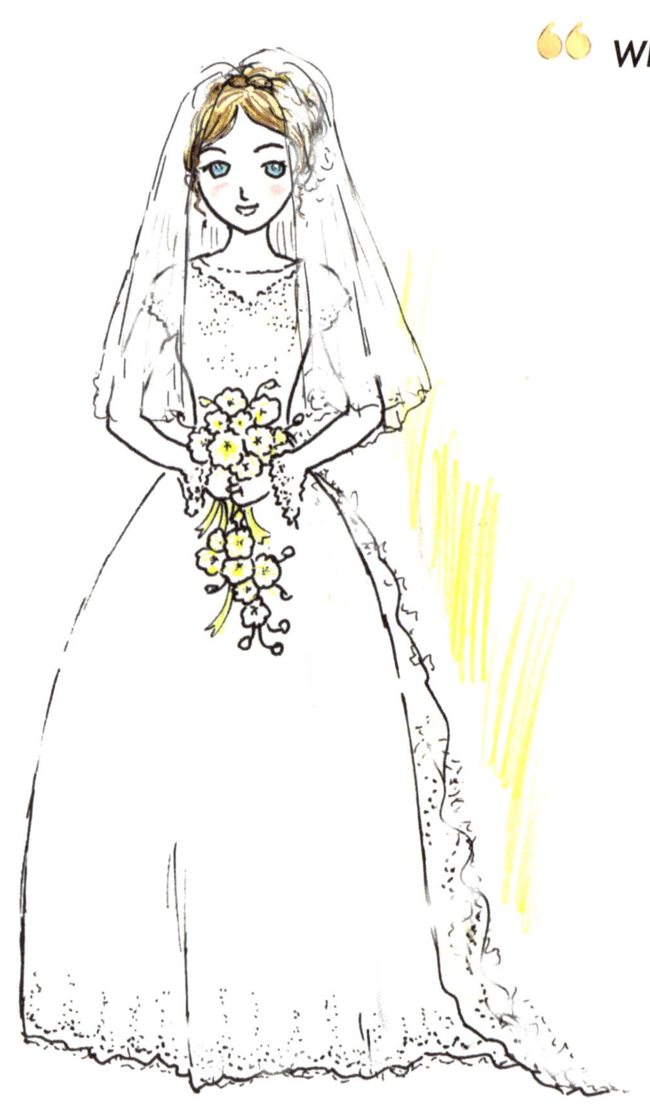

What kinds of kimonos are worn

for wedding ceremonies?

ANSWER 4

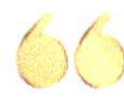 *There are several kinds of kimonos worn at wedding ceremonies.*

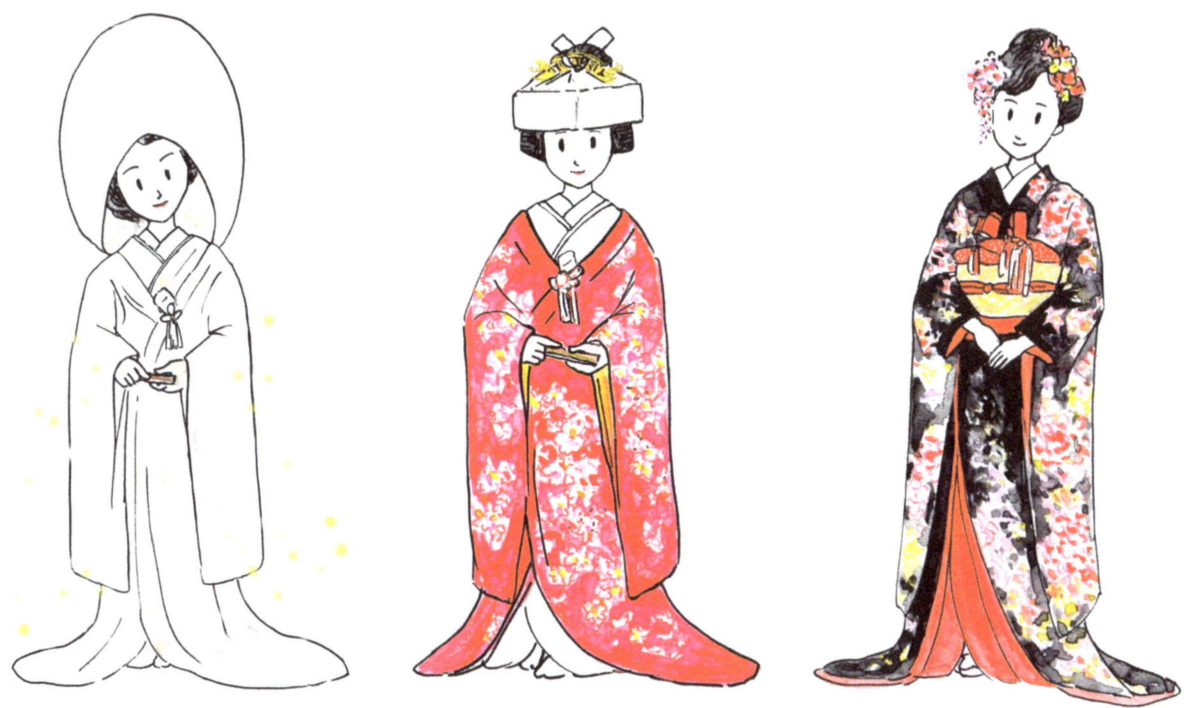

It is common to see wedding processions at shrines and wedding venues.
Kimonos for brides are usually one of the following three kinds:

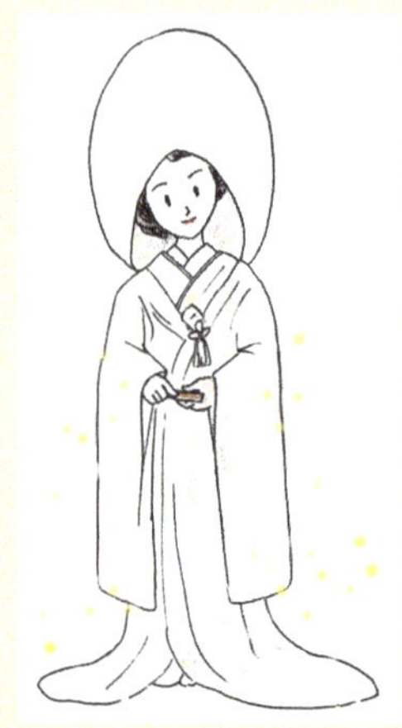

Picture 1: *Shiro-muku:* white wedding kimono
This is the oldest and one of the most formal wedding kimonos. It is exclusively for brides.
It started as a wedding kimono for the brides of ruling class people around the 14th century. All accompanying items, including underwear and small accessories, are white.
A uniquely shaped hat called wata-boushi is an established accessory for this kimono.

Picture 1: *Shiro-muku*

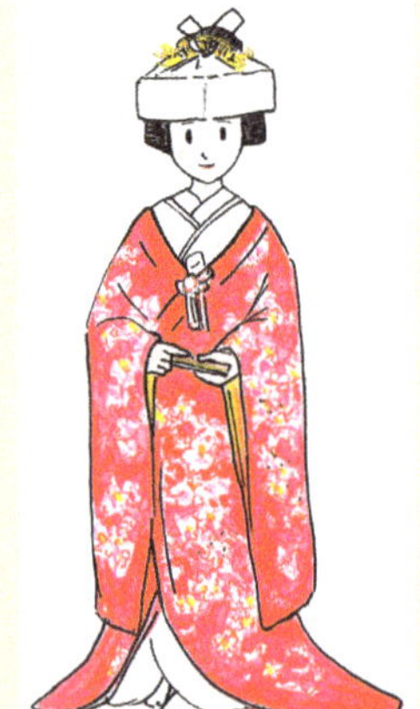

Picture 2: *Iro-uchikake:* wedding kimono
This is also one of the most formal wedding kimonos.
It started as a formal kimono for ruling class people a little later than Shiro-muku. Because of this kimono's beauty, it became prevalent among wealthy merchant families, too.
A unique hat called tsuno-kakushi is an established accessory for this kimono. The meaning of the hat's name is "to hide horns." In Japan, horns imply demons called oni, who easily get angry and scary. In this meaning, this hat implies that a bride "hides horns" and shows only her kind face, without any anger, on her wedding day.

Picture 2: *Iro-uchikake*

Picture 3: *Hiki-furisode*: wedding kimono
This is another wedding kimono exclusively for brides, characterized by long sleeves.
Around the 18th and 19th centuries, this kimono became a popular wedding kimono among high-ranked people, along with a hat called tsuno-kakushi. As this kimono is much longer than a regular kimono, the bottom part is designed with a thick hem. There is a beautiful obi sash (Chapter 6) on the back of this kimono.

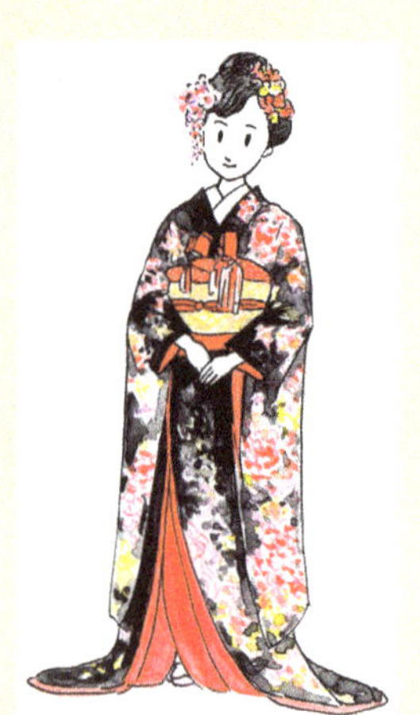

Picture 3: *Hiki-furisode*

2) Maiko kimonos

QUESTION 5

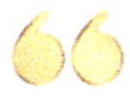 *What is a **maiko**?* 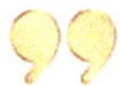

ANSWER 5

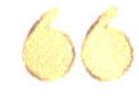 **A maiko is a trainee of Geiko, professional female entertainers. They sing songs and dance at classy Japanese restaurants, especially in Kyoto.**

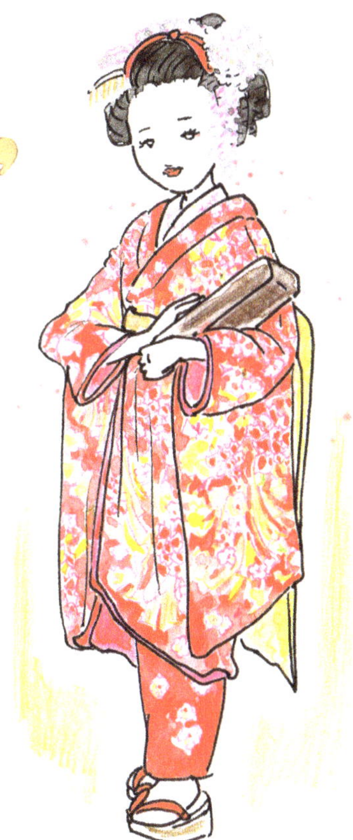

Maiko are trained in etiquette, traditional culture, singing, dancing, and playing instruments. They wear specially made traditional kimonos, which are generally produced in Kyoto.

After they become fully qualified professionals, they are called *Geiko*.

In Eastern Japan, *Geisha* is a term equivalent to *Geiko*. Unlike *maiko*, *Geisha* usually wear kimonos produced in Eastern Japan. There are many shops where people can enjoy a *maiko* kimono experience in Kyoto.

CHAPTER 3

Traditional Kimonos for Ceremonies

After being initially introduced in Japan, kimonos were uniquely developed according to people's lifestyles. Because of this, the styles of kimono vary according to the time period. Until the middle of the 19th century, Japan had limited exchange with Western countries for more than 200 years. Japanese people wore Japanese attire every day until the country was officially opened in the 19th century.

Japan was ruled by warriors called *samurai* from the 12th century to the middle of the 19th century. Current traditional kimono standards of dress were established by the *samurai* class people.

Western standards of dress emphasize time, place, and occasion. Now, Japanese people have a strong understanding of Western attire. After Japan opened the country in the 19th century, the government officially adopted Western dress for public occasions, especially for men. After that, men's kimonos were mainly worn for private events, even though the kimono was in the full formal style.

This is one of the reasons that Japanese men wear kimonos less than women in the ceremonial occasions. As a result, it is challenging to accurately compare the Japanese kimono and Western attire.

In this way, the basis of Japanese kimono dress codes (season, place, occasion) and Western standards of dress (time, place, occasion) are different.

However, to help readers understand the Japanese kimono, I have identified comparisons with Western attire.

1) Traditional formal kimonos for men

QUESTION 6

" What does a formal kimono for men look like? "

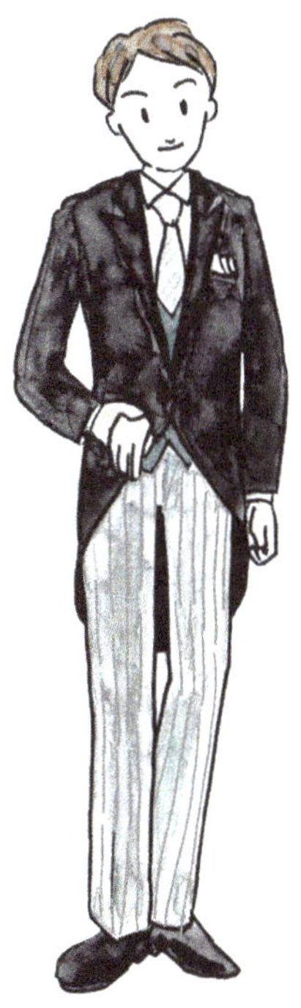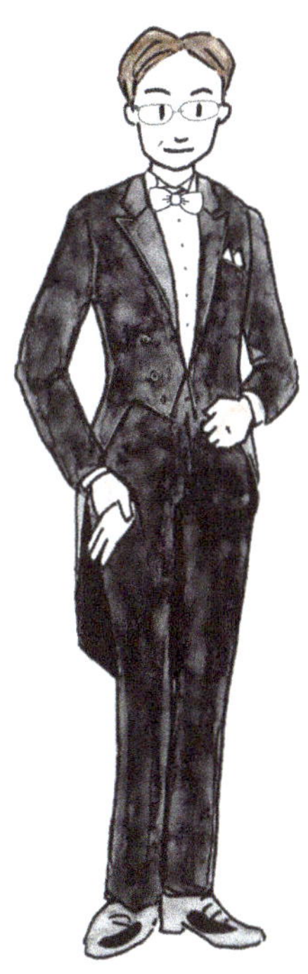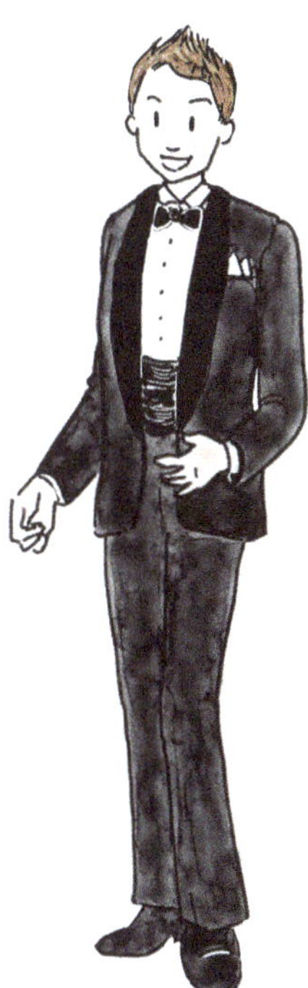

ANSWER 6

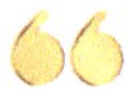 *A formal kimono for men is shown below.* 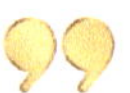

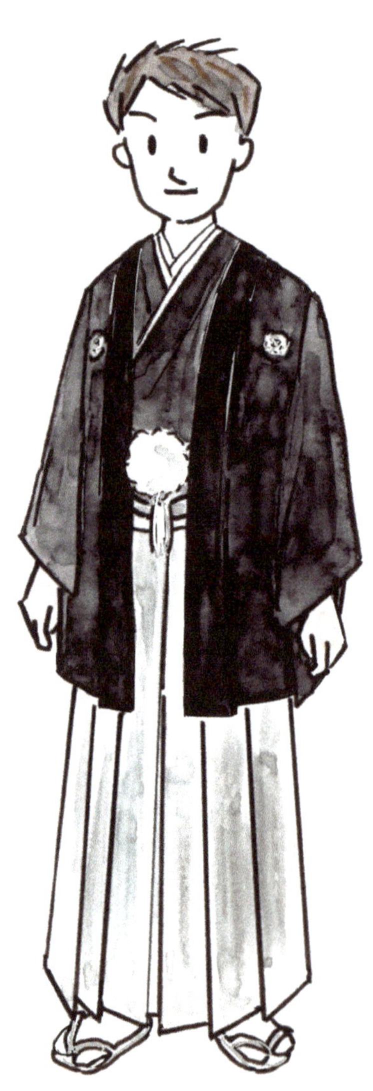

QUESTION 7

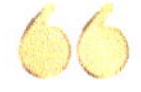 *Western formal wear can be classified by the kind of tie.*

How can we identify the most formal kimonos for men? 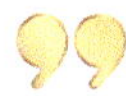

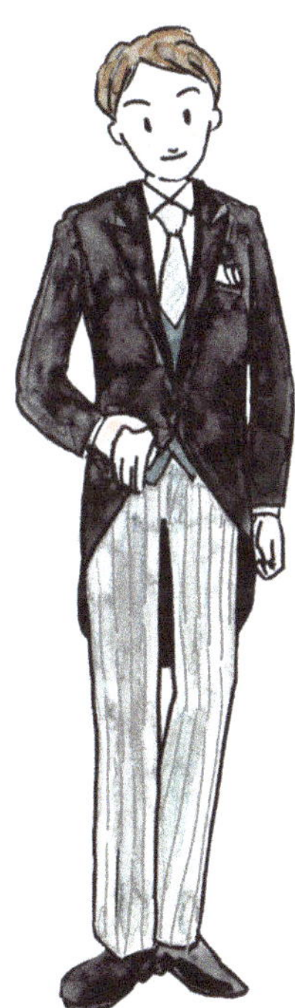 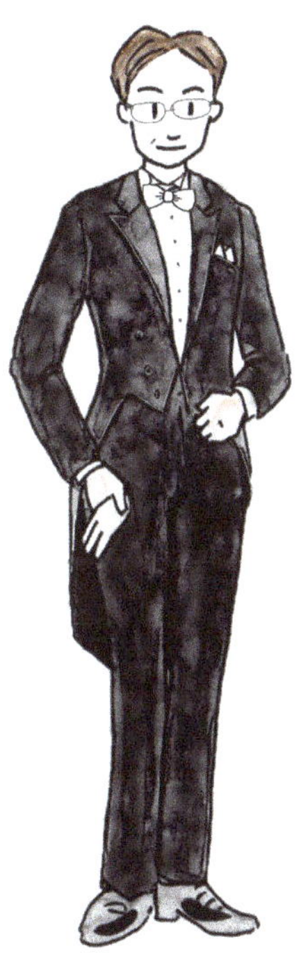 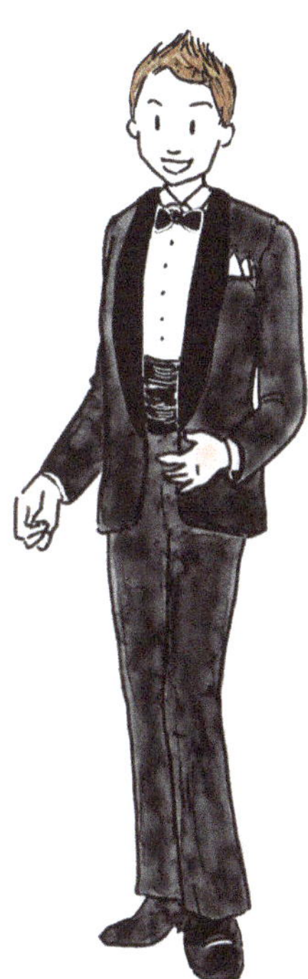

ANSWER 7

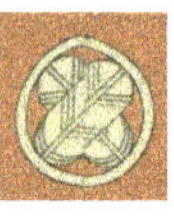

These are family crests, called mon.

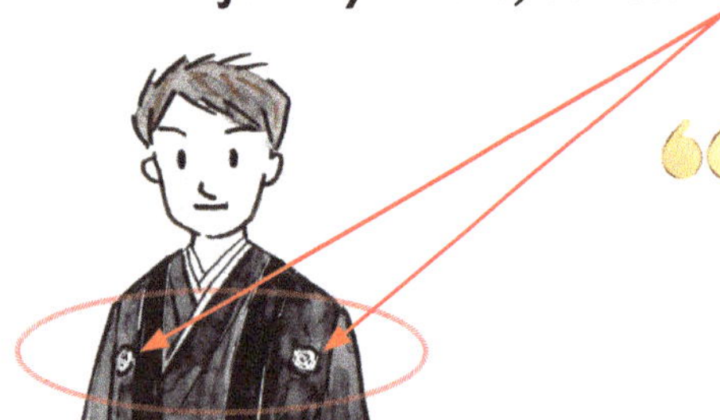

*The most formal kimonos have five **mon**.*
***Mon** to Japanese kimono are*
like ties to Western attire.

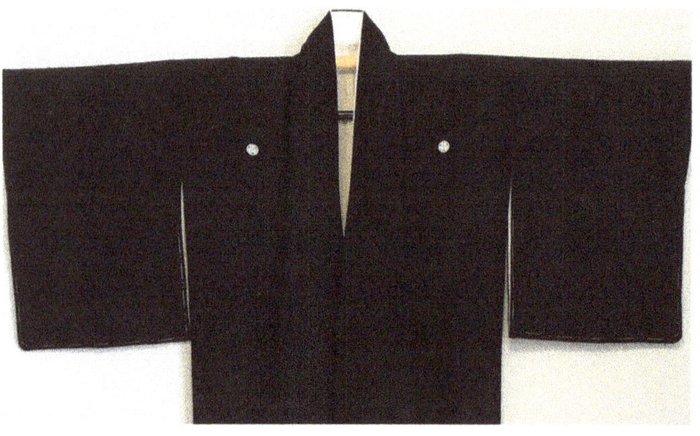

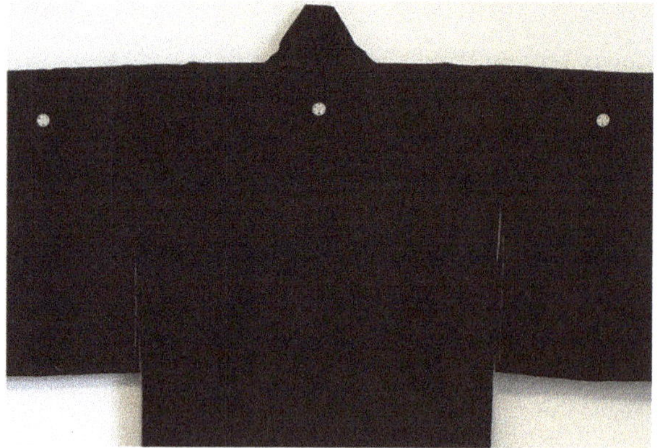

Classifications of traditional kimonos for men are much simpler than those for women.

The points for classification are **materials, weaving and dyeing techniques, colors, and *mon***. When the material is a high-quality **black silk** made with traditional weaving and dyeing techniques, the kimono is considered the most formal style. ***Mon* are family crests** attached to the kimono, and the number of *mon* attached is determined according to the rank of the kimono (see a table in the next page).

***Mon* are regarded similarly to ties in Western attire, such as white ties and black ties.** There are strict rules for *mon* for both men's and women's kimonos, so, *mon* are the best features to determine the classification of a formal kimono. The most formal kimonos have five *mon*: two *mon* on the front and three *mon* on the back.

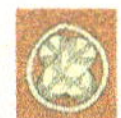 *Mon*: family crests on kimonos which function similar to ties in Western attire

WESTERN CLOTHES	KIMONO
Formal attire	**Five *mon*** The most formal kimonos for both men and women have five *mon*, which are dyed to fabric using the most advanced technique. The positions for *mon* are strictly determined. The most formal women's kimonos (*kuro-tomesode* P22) always have five *mon*. Women can choose the number of *mon* for the second-most formal type of kimono (*iro-tomesode* P25) when they tailor the kimono.
Semiformal attire	**Three *mon*** Three *mon* are used for semiformal kimonos for both men and women. *Mon* are attached to the back and sleeves. The second-most formal type of women's kimonos (*iro-tomesode* P25) often have three *mon*.
Informal attire	**One *mon*** One *mon* is used for semiformal or informal kimonos for men and women. When a kimono has only one *mon*, it is considered less formal than kimonos with three *mon*. The *mon* is often attached to the back of the kimono.

This table shows a traditional Japanese classification of *mon*. Currently this classification is relaxed in international ceremonies. Additionally, there are some exceptions such as women's formal kimono *furisode* (P26) and semiformal kimono *houmongi* (P34), which usually don't have *mon*.

There are several stories about the origin of *mon*. One of them is that *mon* started around the 10th or 11th century among the court nobles in Japan as a family crest to recognize their belongings. Later, *samurai* warriors began using their family crests to determine their allies and enemies during battle. After the 19th century, ordinary people officially started using surnames, and *mon* as family crests became more common.

Different from traditional *mon* in this table, there are casual *mon*, which are called *sharemon*. They have totally different concepts behind them and are much more casual.

2) *Tomesode*: Traditional formal kimonos for women

QUESTION 8

*A wedding procession is passing by.
Is it possible to determine who the
mothers of the bride and the groom are?*

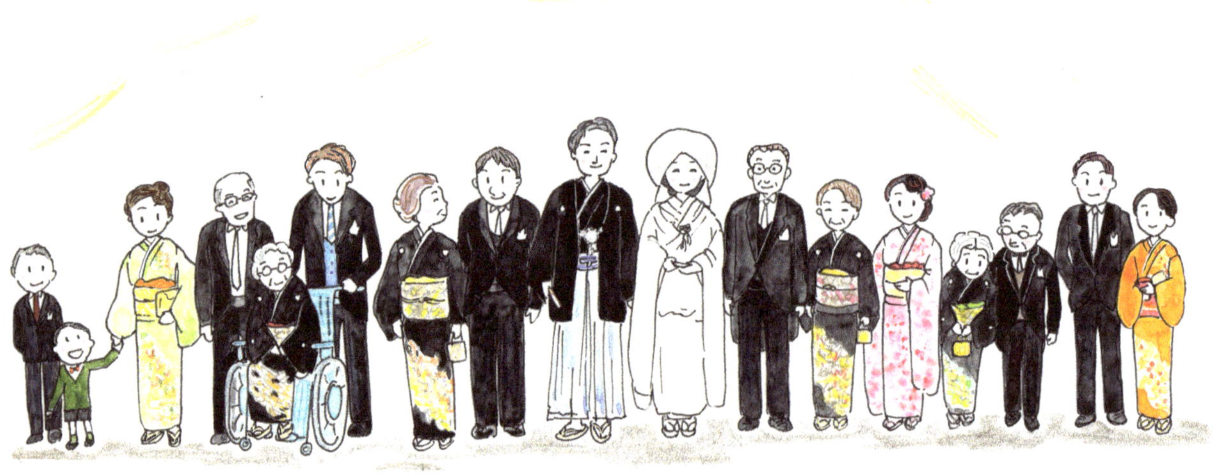

ANSWER 8

❝ *The mothers and grandmothers of the bride and groom wear gorgeous black kimonos (**kuro-tomesode**) in a wedding ceremony.* ❞

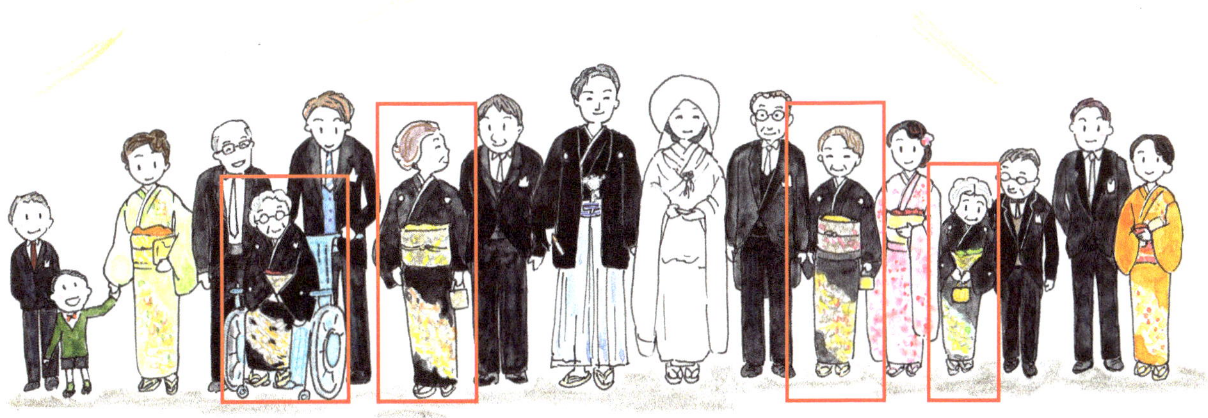

Groom's grandmother and mother   Bride's mother and grandmother

Tomesode: **Tradtional formal kimonos for women**

Traditional kimonos for women have short sleeves, typically 49 cm long. When they are made, the patterns, techniques, and *mon* (P20) are determined according to specific rules.

Tomesode can be black or colored. Black *tomesode* are usually considered to be the most formal kimonos.

Black type *(kuro-tomesode)*

Specific people wear specific types of kimonos on formal occasions. For example, the mothers of the bride and groom wear a *kuro-tomesode* kimono at wedding ceremonies. It should have five *mon,* dyed using the most advanced technique.

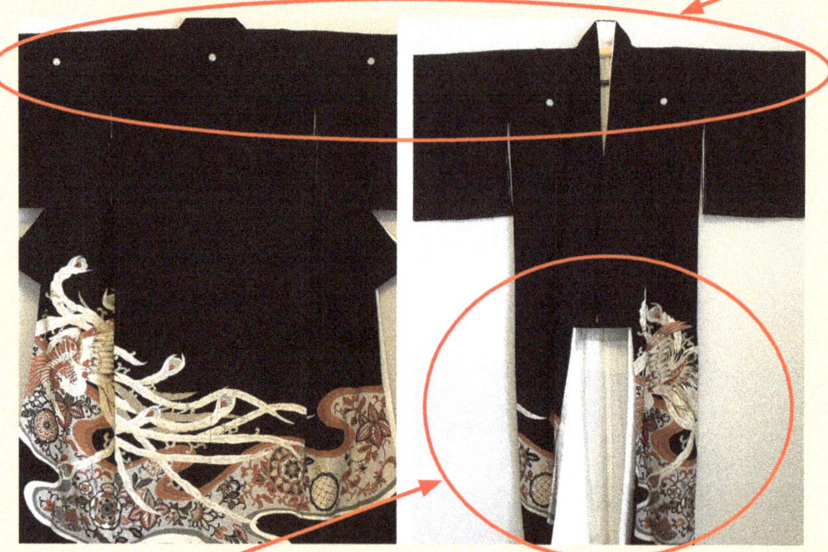

1. Patterns are considered auspicious and are dyed or embroidered only on the skirt of the kimono.
2. Linings of hems should be made from the same cloth as the front cloth.
3. There is also a white silk inner cloth to make some parts double layered.
4. Silk cloth is woven with a specific technique.
5. *Obi* sashes (P79) have a gold or silver base and are ornamented with auspicious patterns.

Colored type (*iro-tomesode*)

These are usually considered as either the most formal or the second-most formal kimonos for women. **The points used to classify formal kimonos are *mon* and auspicious patterns.**

Iro-tomesode kimonos can be regarded as the same rank as the black type (*kuro-tomesode*) only if they have five *mon*.

The colored type can be worn on a wider variety of occasions than the black type, because people can choose the number of *mon*. For example, because this kimono has five *mon*, it can be regarded as the same rank as the black type.

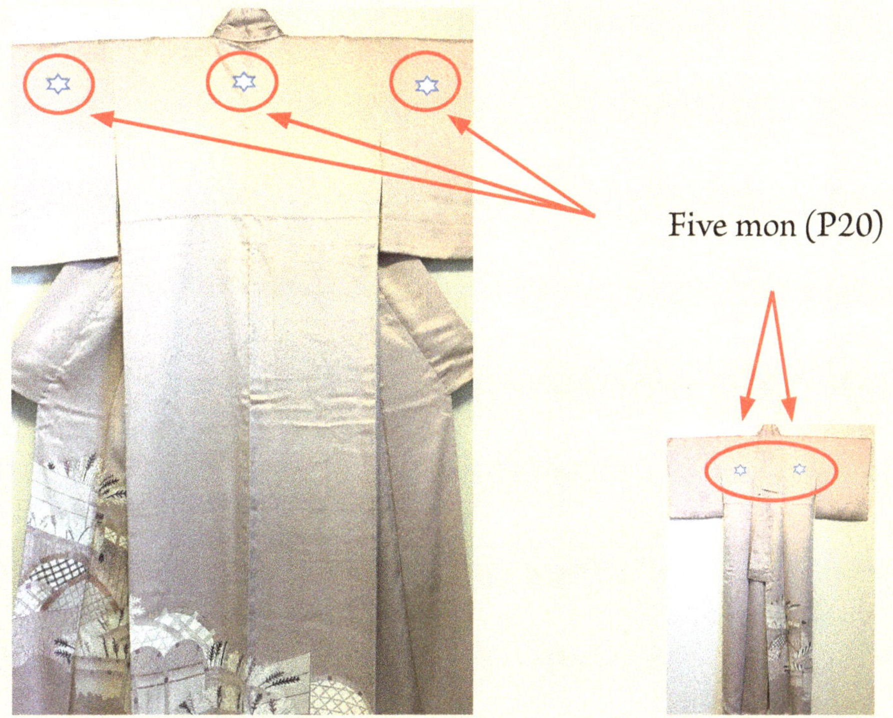

This *iro-tomesode* kimono was made for attending imperial events. Although the black type (*kuro-tomesode*) are regarded as the most formal kimonos, they are avoided at imperial events. It is more common to see this colored type in international ceremonies.

3) *Furisode:* Traditional formal kimonos for young single women

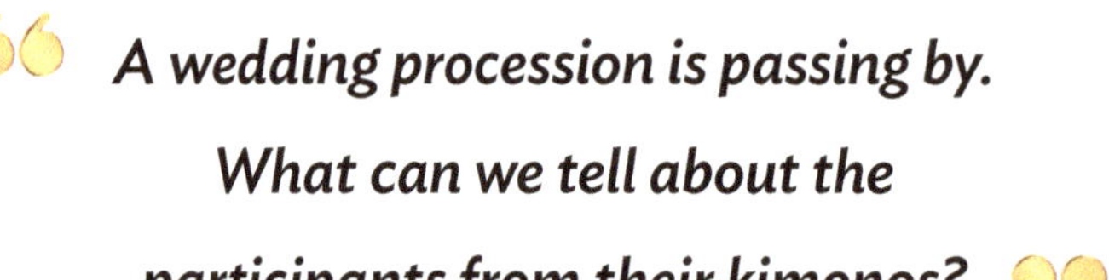

A wedding procession is passing by.
What can we tell about the
participants from their kimonos?

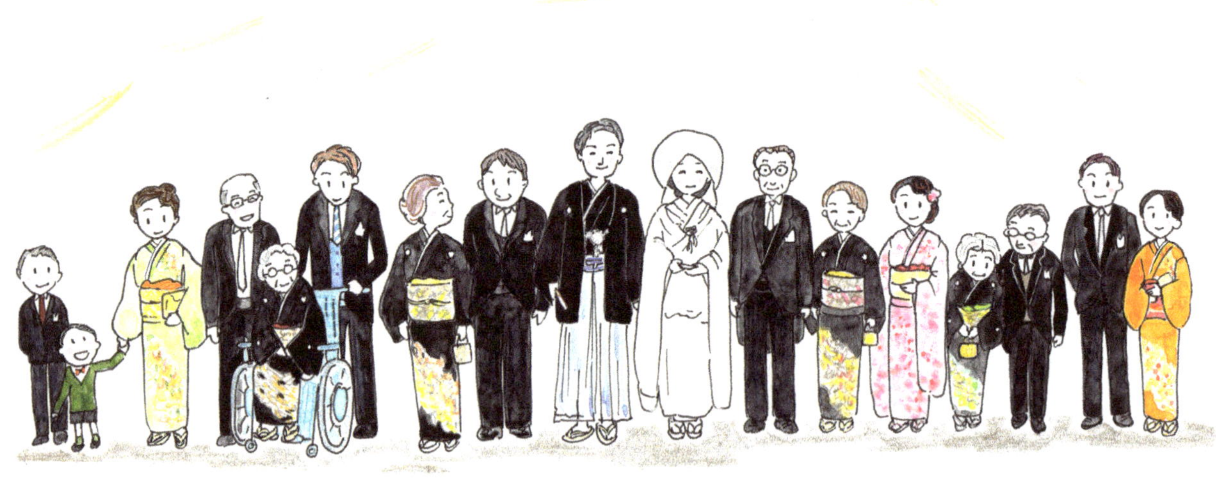

ANSWER 9

*Young single women wear kimonos with long sleeves (**furisode**). **Furisode** is the most formal kimono style for them.*

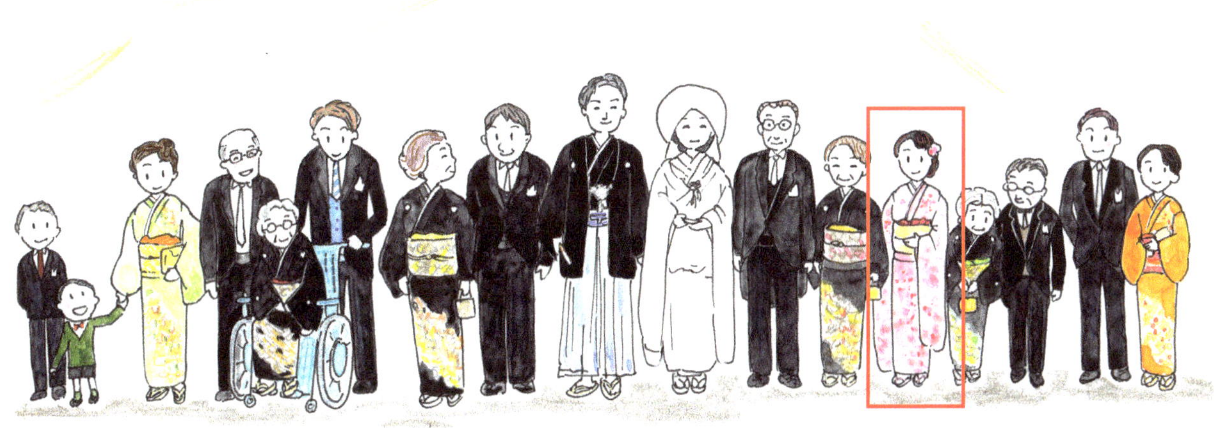

Furisode: Traditional formal kimonos for young single women

Japanese *furisode* are the kimono equivalent of formal Western gowns. These kimonos with long sleeves are the most formal kimono for young single women. *Mon* (P20) are not needed to identify this kimono, as its long sleeves have a very distinct shape. When young single women attend a formal ceremony such as a wedding ceremony, they often wear this kimono.

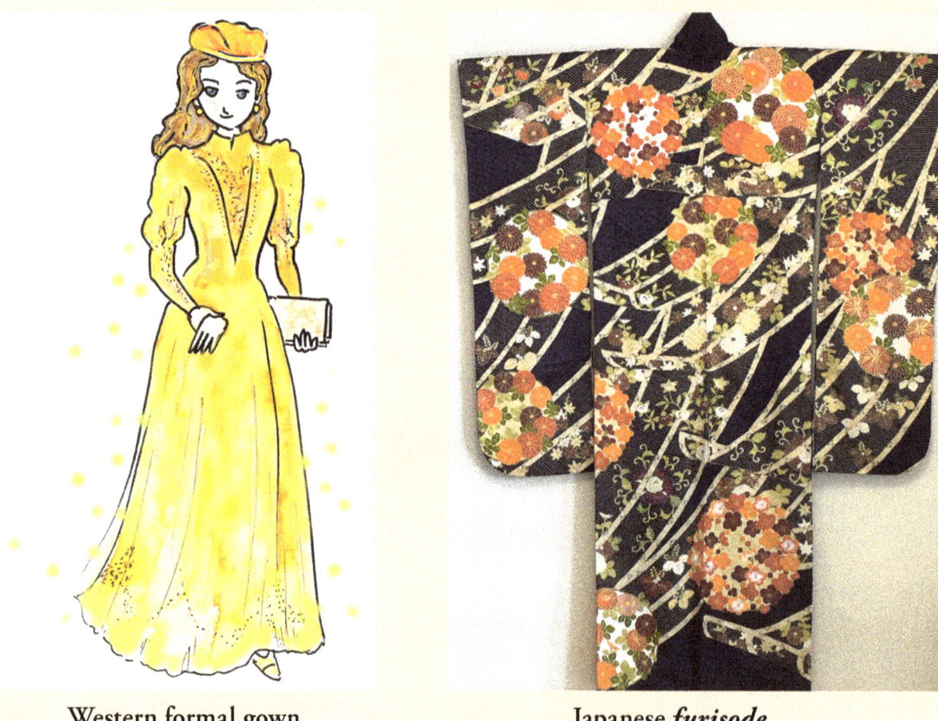

Western formal gown

Japanese *furisode*

Coming-of-Age Ceremony

A traditional Japanese ceremony is an excellent opportunity to wear this kimono.

Many women attend a coming-of-age ceremony on the second Monday of January in the year that they will become a legal adult.

Styling kimonos in the 2000s

Although formal kimonos are expensive, they are treasured within the whole family.

Below is an example of a formal kimono made for a woman for her coming-of-age ceremony several decades ago.

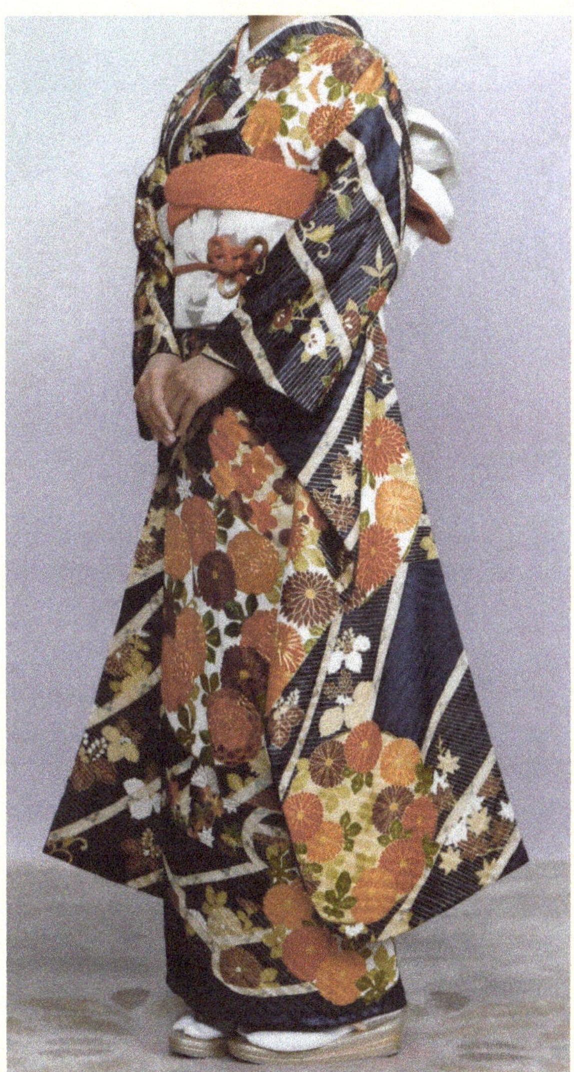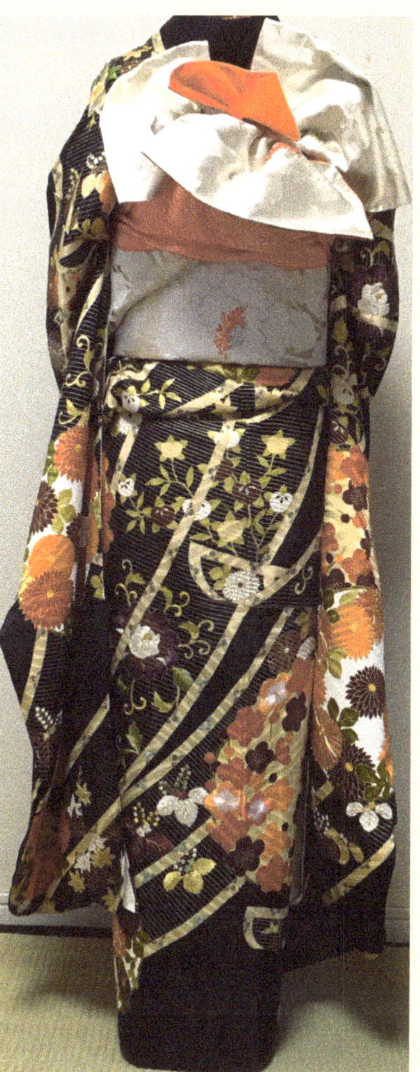

Styling kimonos today

Small accessories are beautifully arranged to match the trends of the time. The kimono below is the same kimono shown on the previous page, worn in the coming-of-age ceremony in 2020.

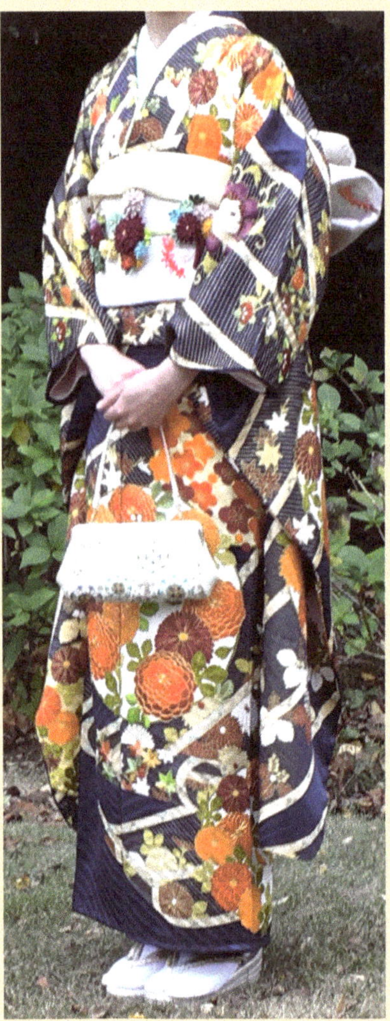
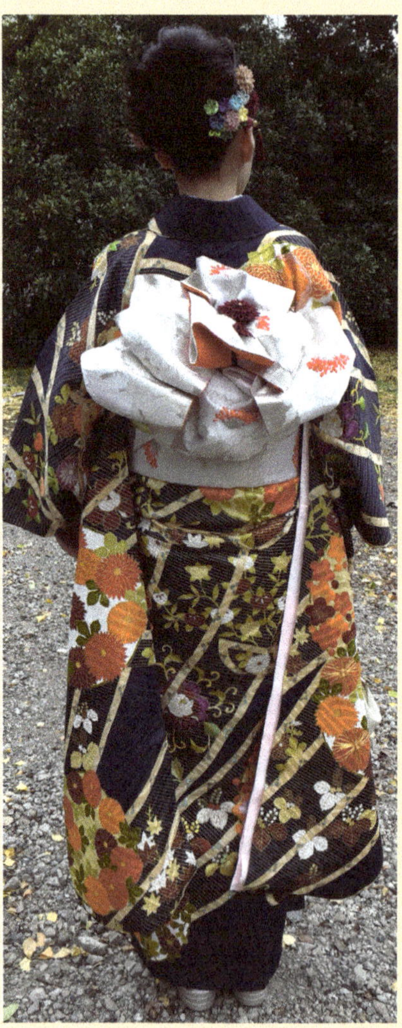

Kimono accessories made by contemporary designers

This coordination was totally designed by a hair and makeup artist, Kiyomi Murakami. She is the first Japanese champion in the WELLA TREND VISION AWARD World Final in Louvre Museum.

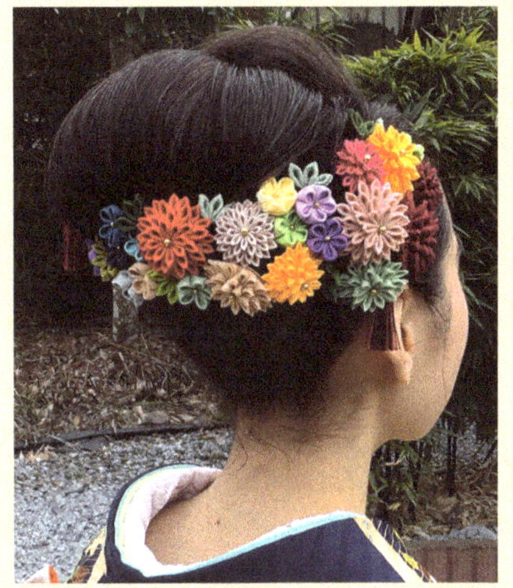
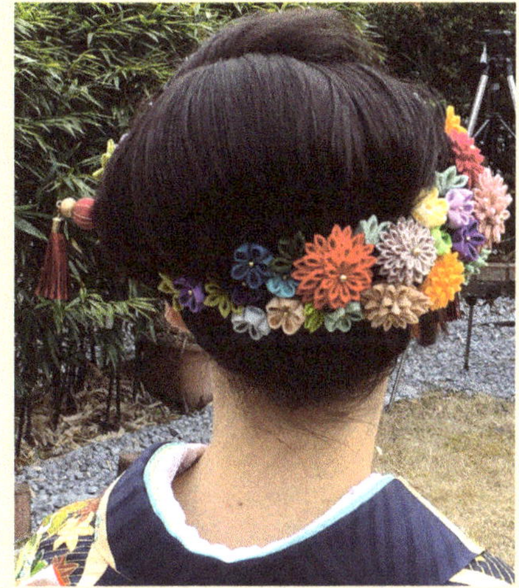

All of these kimono accessories were made by hand. The designers carefully chose each accessory's color according to the kimono colors. For example, sky-blue hair accessories are coordinated with similar *obi* sash accessories, a sky-blue collar, and kimono pattern.

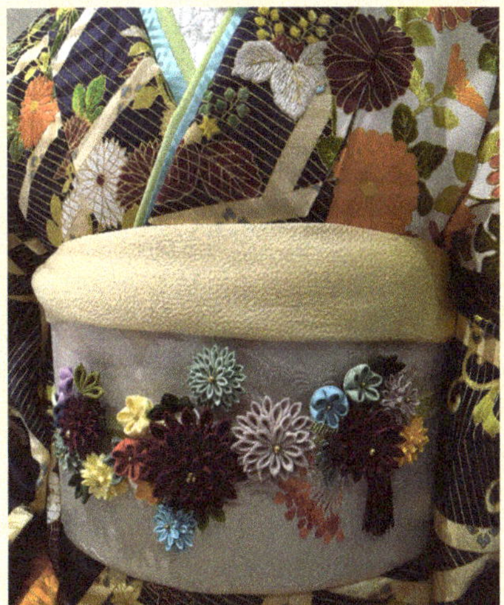
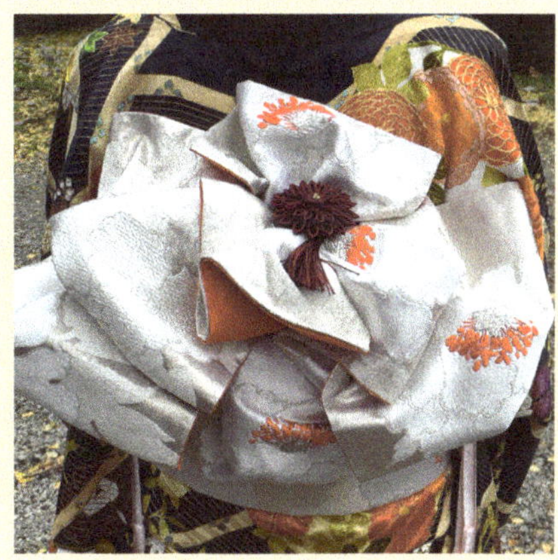

Salon information: Rock paper scissors
Hair and makeup artist: Kiyomi Murakami,
Makeup artist: Nanako Egawa

Kimono accessories made by contemporary designers

Kimono accessories can be coordinated with the color of the kimono and *obi* sash. The theme of the color coordination is often nature.

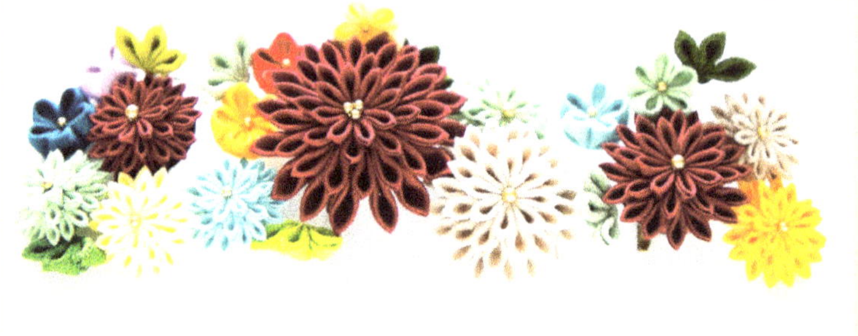

An accessory designer's information

Name: ayatsumami

Instagram: ayatsumami

This Japanese accessory is called *Tsumamizaiku.*

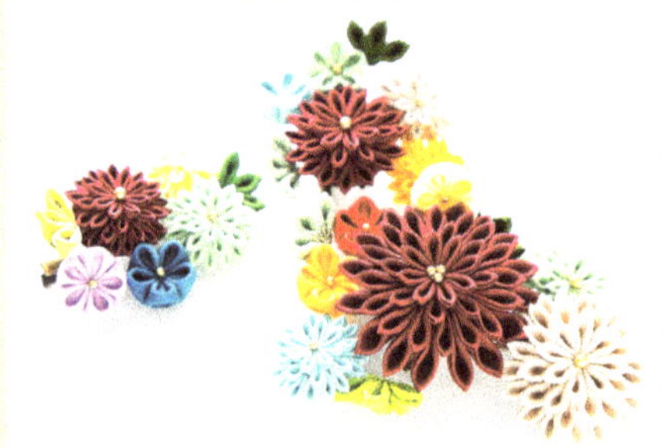

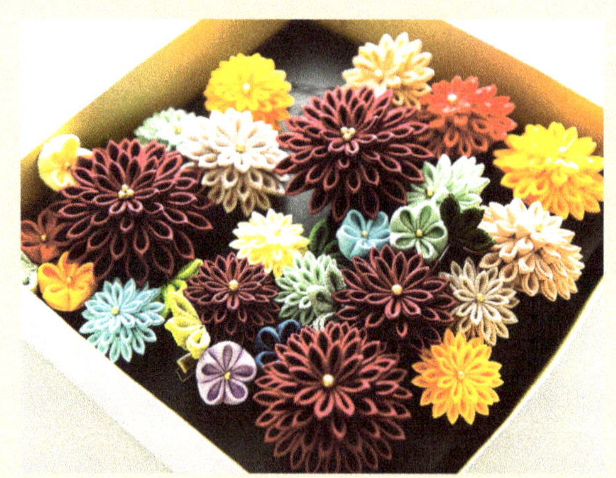

A fabric jewelry designer's information

Name: Sextile

Instagram: Sextile.jp

Online shop: Creema

https://www.creema.jp/c/sextile/item/onsale

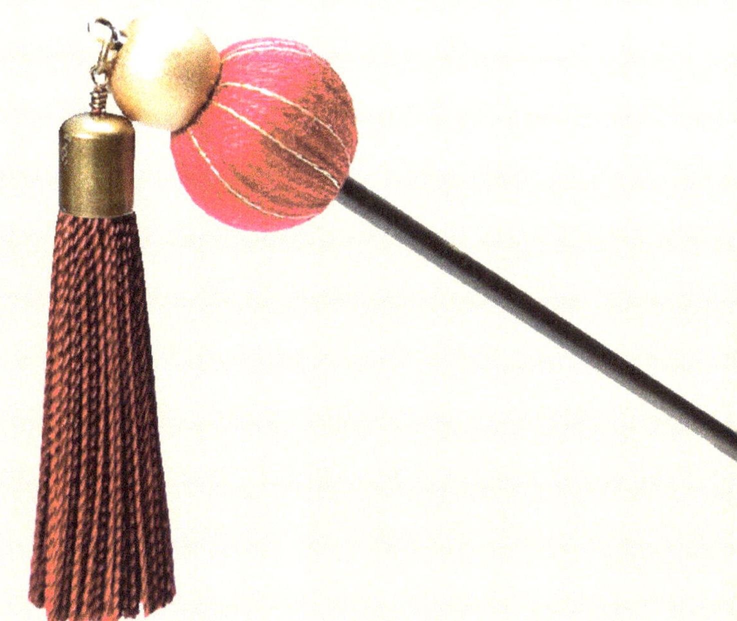

4) *Houmongi*: Traditional semiformal kimonos for women

QUESTION 10

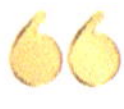 *A wedding procession is passing by.*

Which kimonos are considered semiformal? 

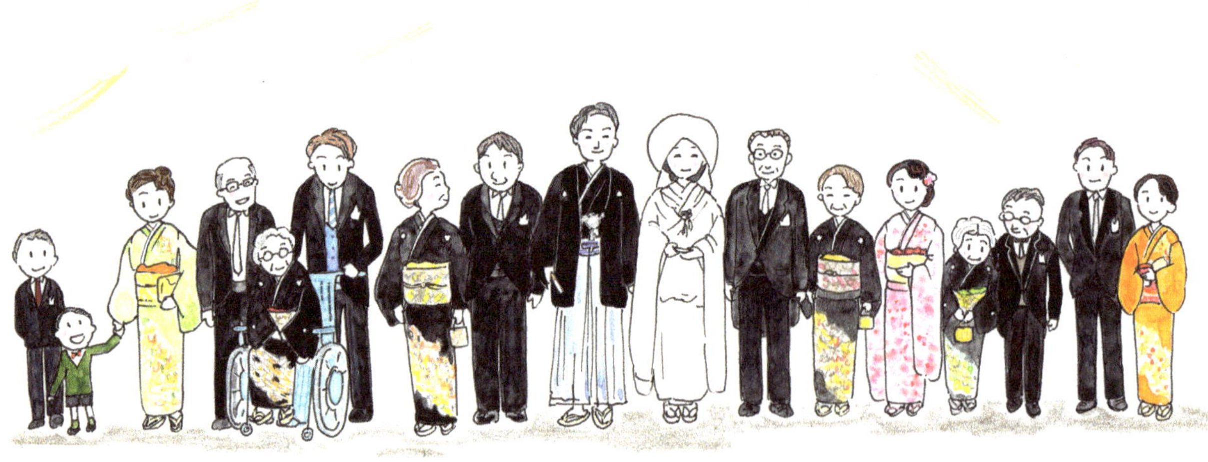

ANSWER 10

> *Kimonos worn by women at wedding ceremonies are often semiformal kimonos.* **Houmongi** *are traditional semiformal kimonos, equivalent to semiformal Western dresses.*

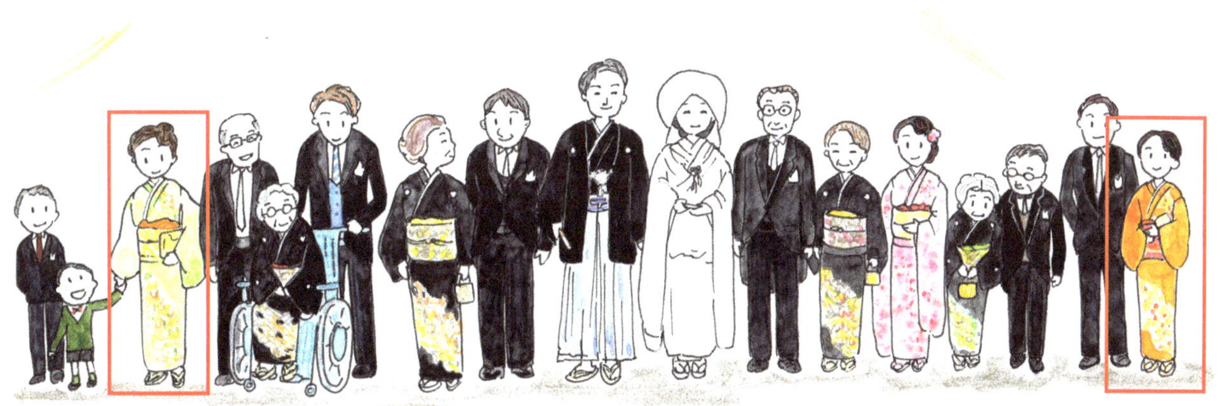

Groom's relative or friend

Bride's relative or friend

Houmongi: Traditional semiformal kimonos for women

This kimono features auspicious designs that appear as a single, cohesive image. Patterns are located only around the breast and the skirt of the kimono.

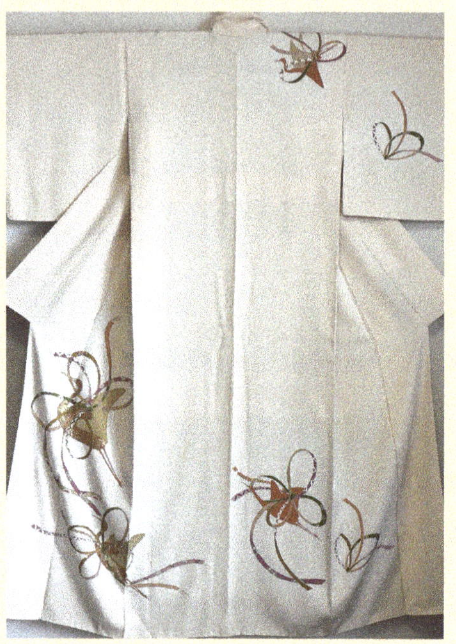

The process to make this kimono is essential. To make this cohesive picture, first, white silk material cloth is sewn and fitted to the wearer.

After the design is decided, it is taken apart into fabric pieces to dye according to the design.

Thanks to this process, the design is seamless, and the whole kimono looks like one beautiful picture.

It is an elegant kimono suitable for a variety of ceremonies.

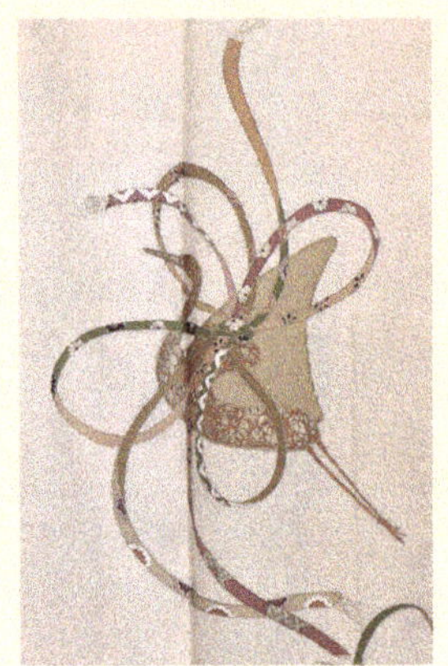
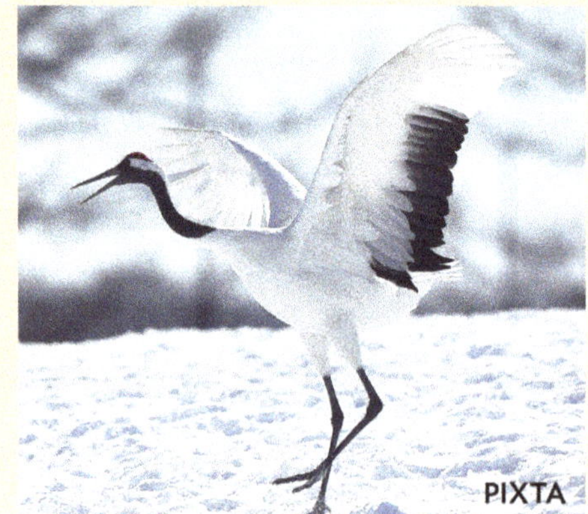

In Japan, cranes are regarded as a symbol of happiness because of their longevity. *Houmongi* usually do not have *mon*.

5) Traditional formal and semiformal kimonos for women

QUESTION 11

❝ *How can you distinguish women's traditional formal kimonos and semiformal kimonos from other kimonos?* ❞

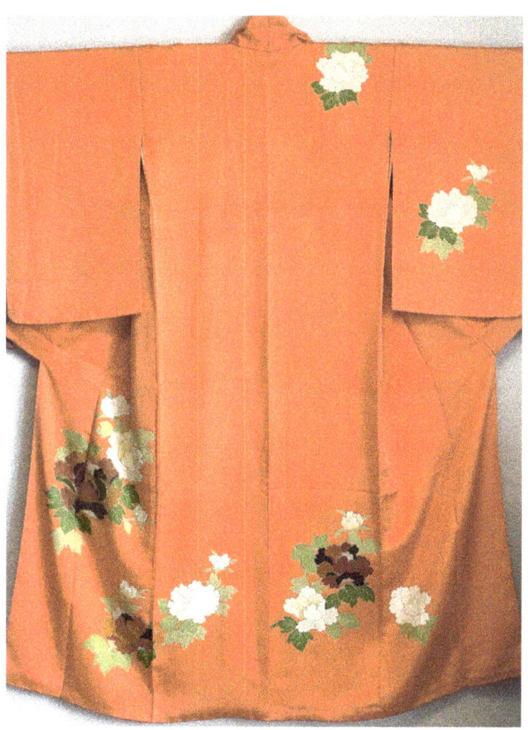

This kimono was originally made for me when I was seven years old to attend a ceremony. Ten years later, it was made into the adult size.

ANSWER 11

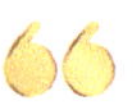 *There are three points used to distinguish women's formal kimonos and semiformal kimonos from others.*

1. *They have **auspicious patterns and colors** suitable to the occasion.*

2. *They have **mon**, similar to men's formal kimonos.*
*   ***Furisode** (P26) and **houmongi** (P34) are exceptions.*

3. *They are made of specific kinds of silk.*
*   *There are some exceptions.*

The traditional kimono follows traditional standards of dress. Similar to Western attire, there are certain standards for kimonos. Men's formal kimonos tend to be simple, while women's are more complicated.

However, by knowing the three points above, it becomes easier to distinguish formal kimonos and semiformal kimonos from others. Just by knowing a few key points to identify the differences, observing kimonos can become much more enjoyable.

Examples of Auspicious Patterns

QUESTION 12

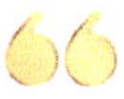 *What does this auspicious kimono*

pattern symbolize?

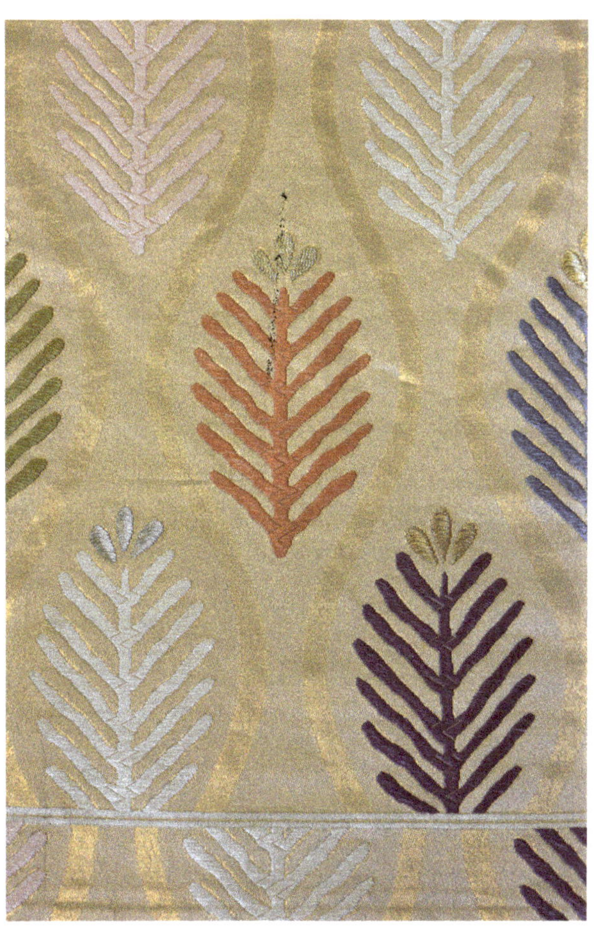

ANSWER 12

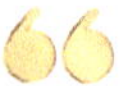 *Pine trees* 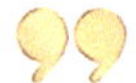

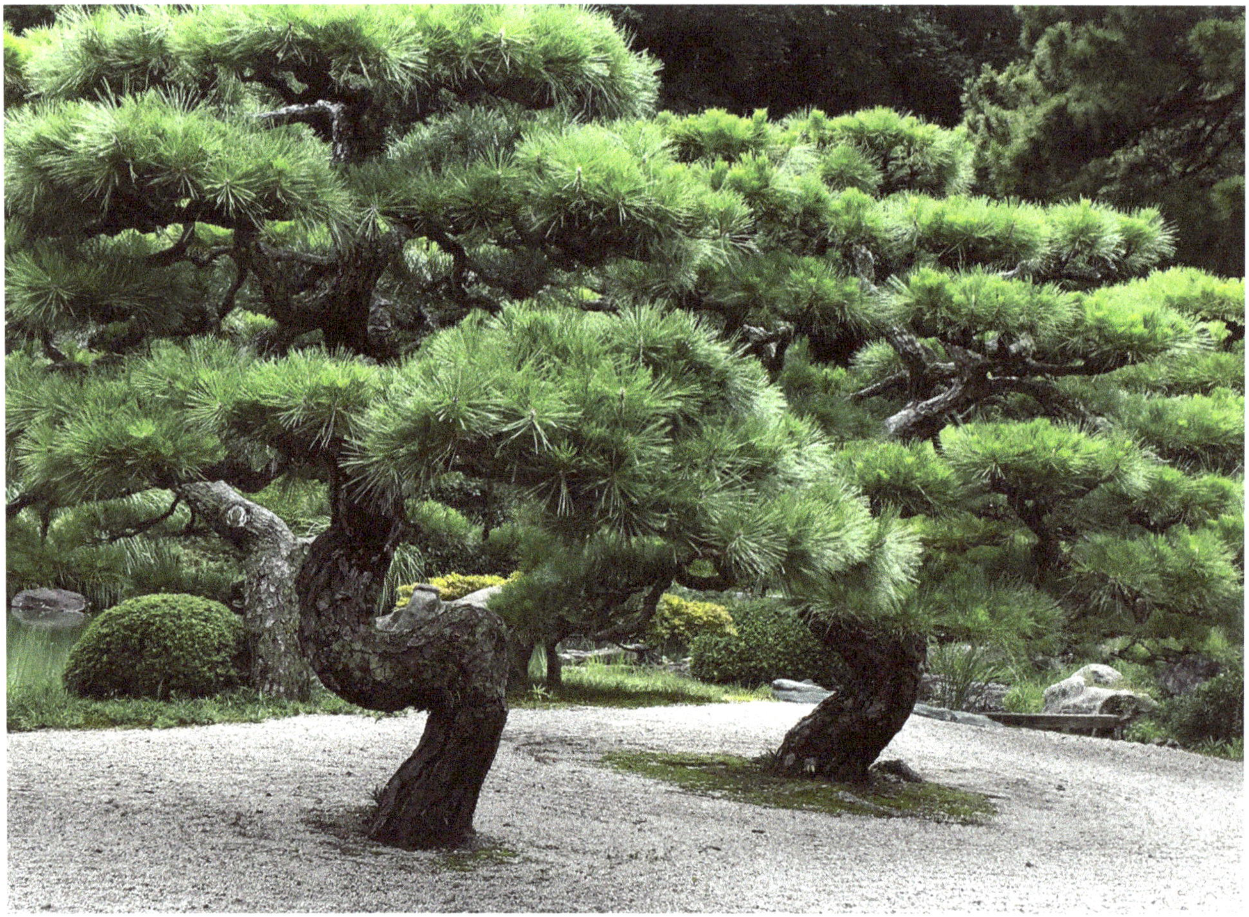

Pine trees remain green throughout the year, even during Japan's cold winter. Because of this, pine tree patterns are regarded as a symbol of happiness.

QUESTION 13

What does this auspicious kimono pattern represent?

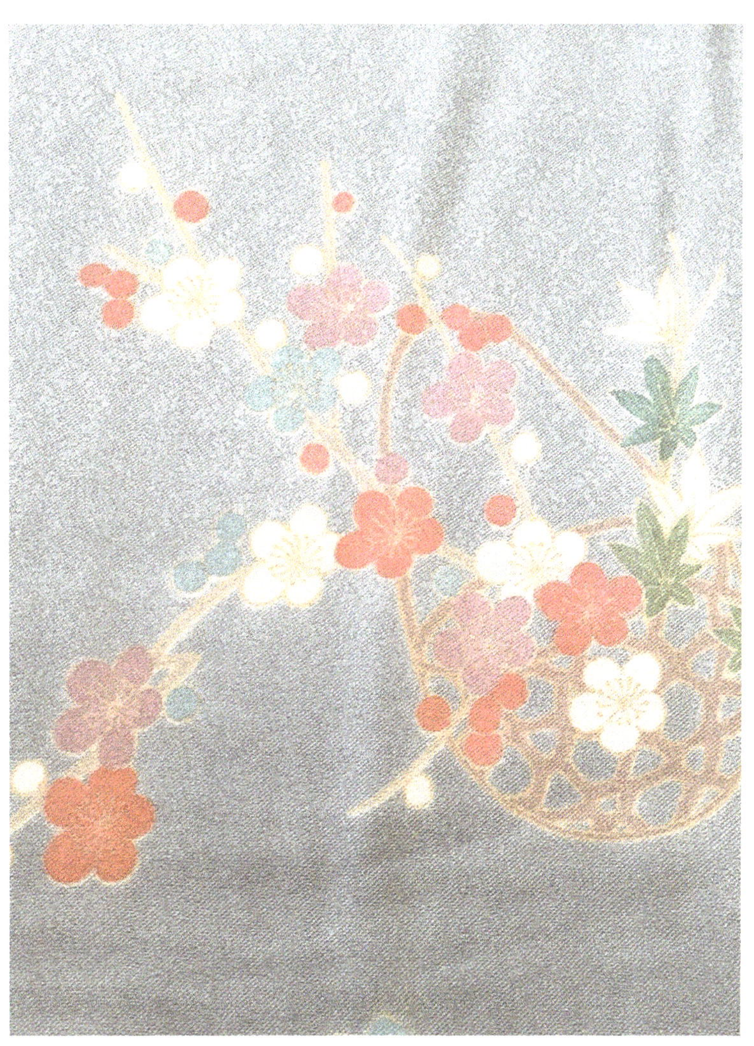

ANSWER 13

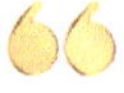 *Plum blossoms* 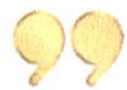

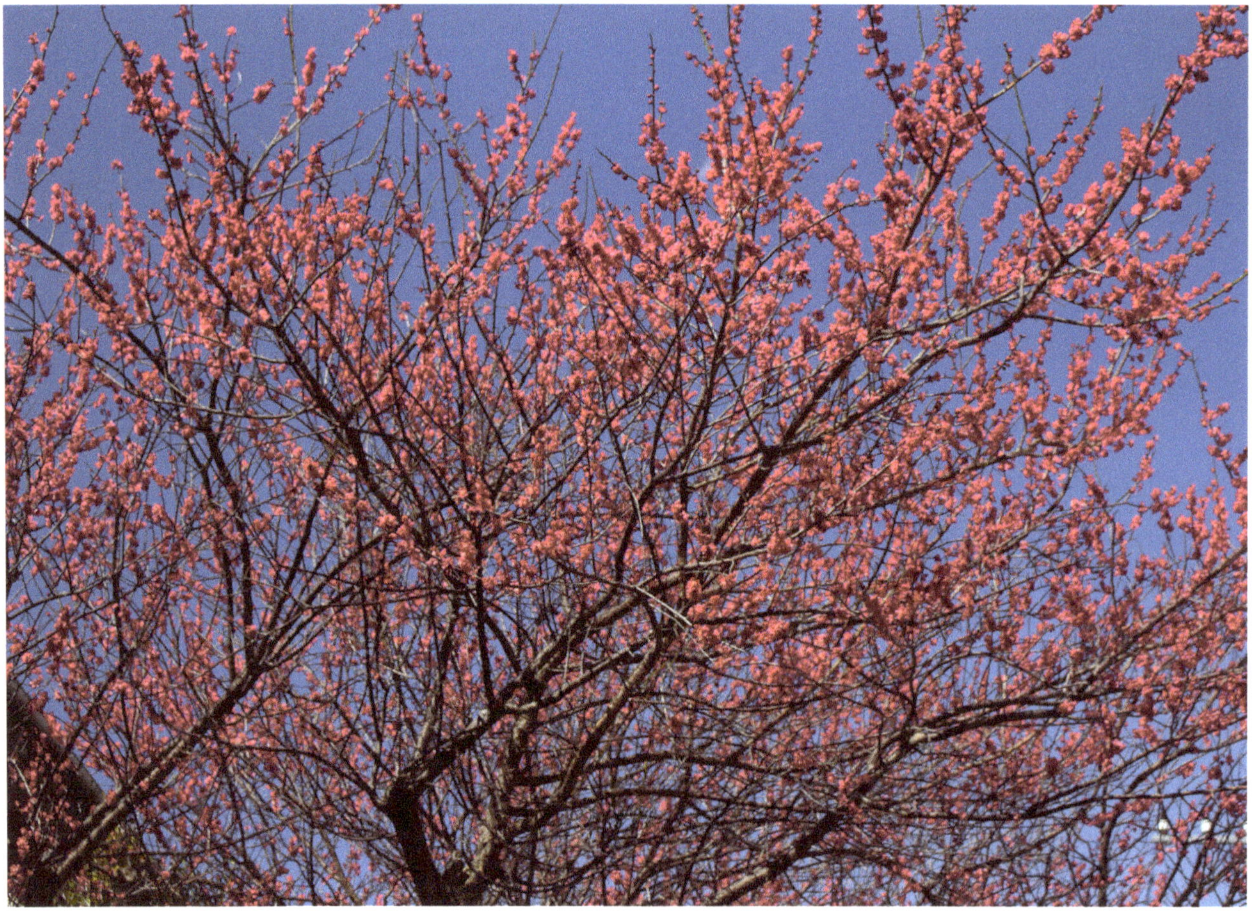

Plum blossoms bloom earlier in the year than other flowers. This is why plum blossom patterns are also regarded as happy symbols, along with pine tree and bamboo patterns.

QUESTION 14

❝ What does this auspicious kimono pattern represent? ❞

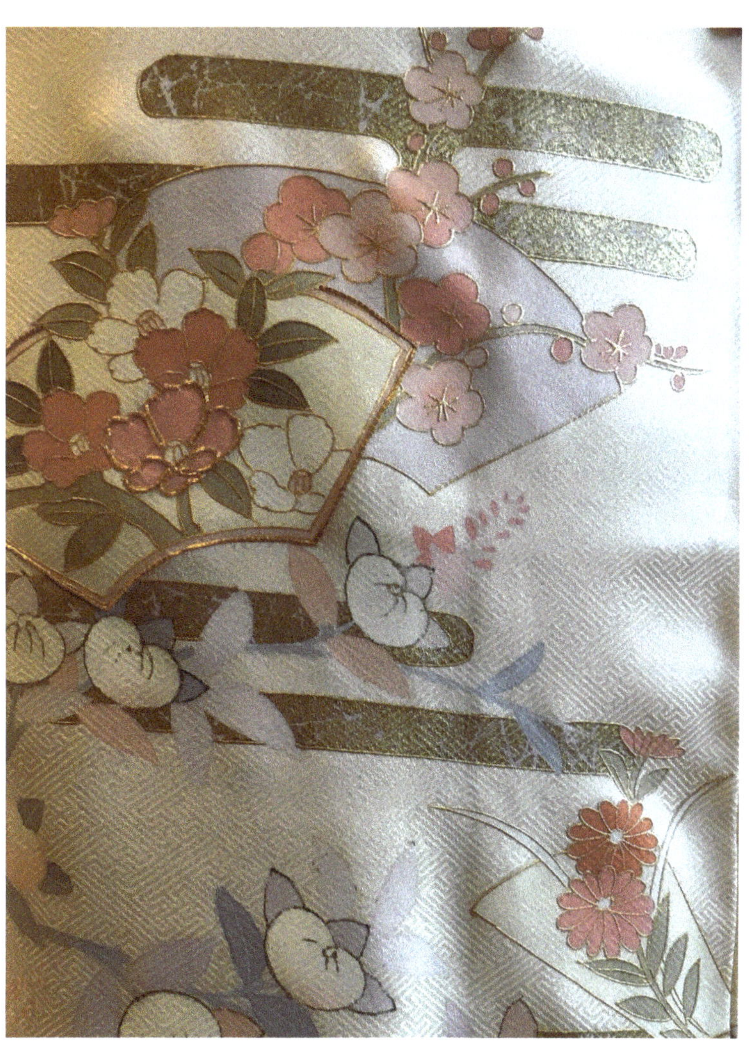

ANSWER 14

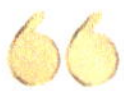 *Folding fans* 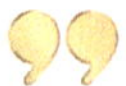

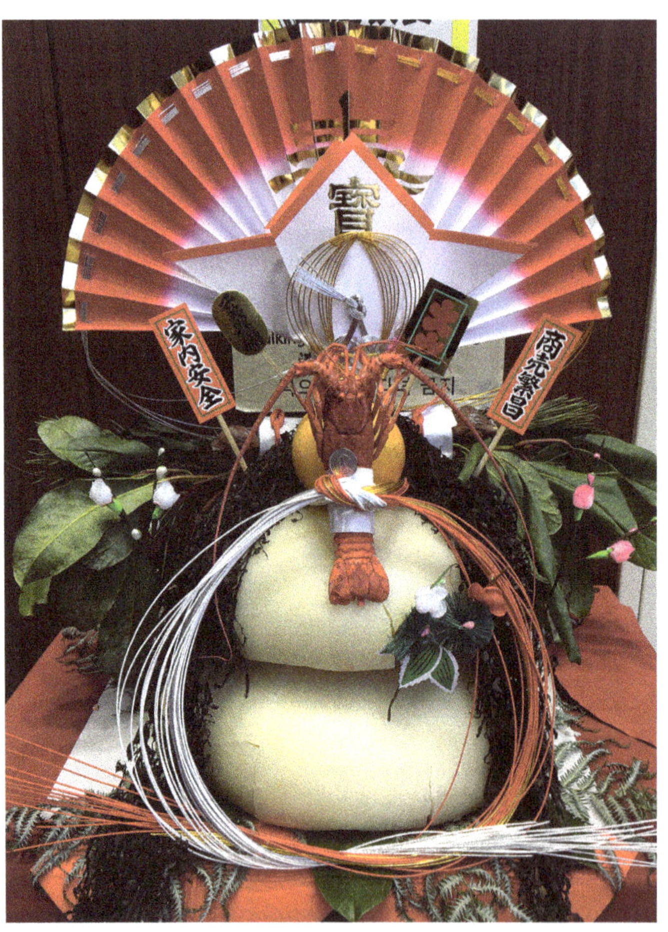

Folding fans are considered to have a happy shape because its ends become wider when opened. In Japan, this widened shape is symbolic of a splendid future. Therefore, they are regarded as a symbol of happiness and prosperity.

Examples of Auspicious Colors

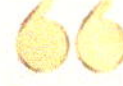 *Red and white* 

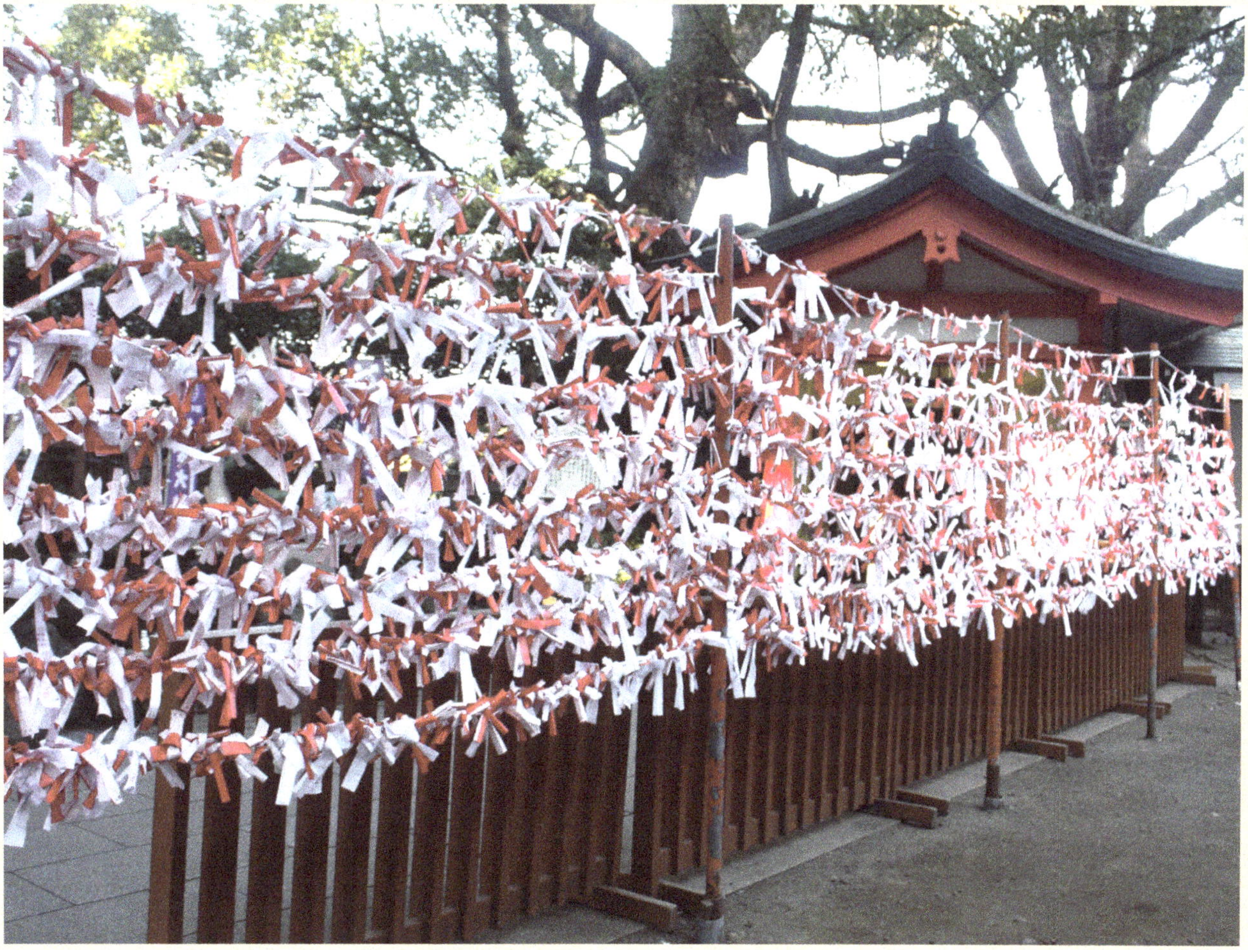

The combination of red and white is regarded as a symbol of happiness, which we can see on many auspicious occasions in Japan.

QUESTION 15

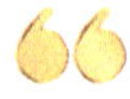 *On what occasions do Japanese women wear formal or semiformal kimonos?* 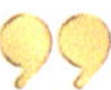

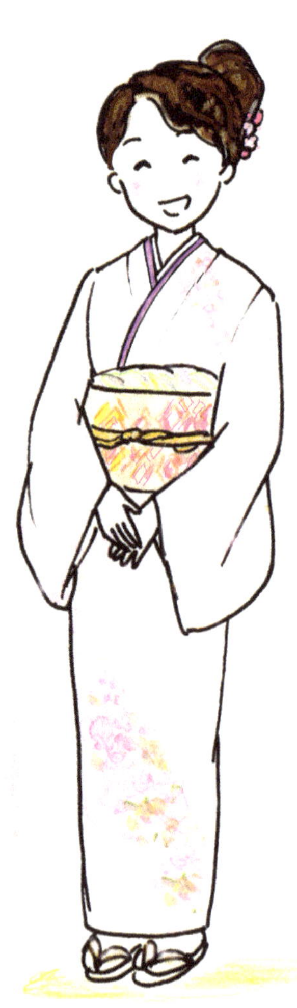

ANSWER 15

> 66 *Japanese women often wear formal or semiformal kimonos at traditional Japanese ceremonies or at annual events.* 99

Example 1: Traditional Japanese Ceremony for Newborn Babies

About 30 days after a baby's birth, parents and grandparents take the baby to a shrine to pray for his or her healthy growth. There are some standards for wearing kimonos at this traditional Japanese ceremony.

- ◇ The baby's mother and grandmothers usually wear semiformal kimonos. (P34, P50)
- ◇ The baby's father and grandfathers usually wear a Western suit. (Reason: P16)
- ◇ Baby's kimono

The person who holds the baby is usually a grandmother.

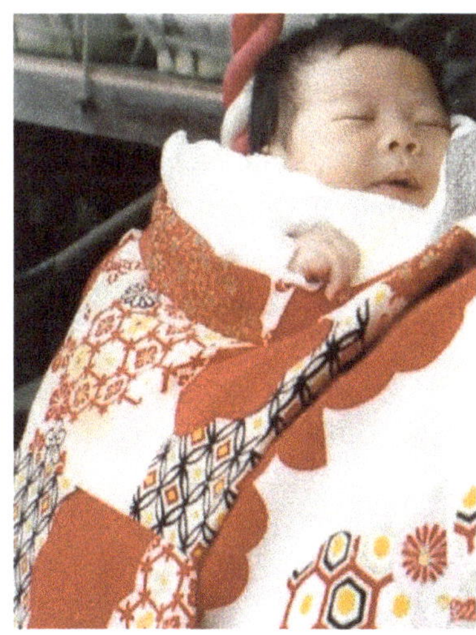

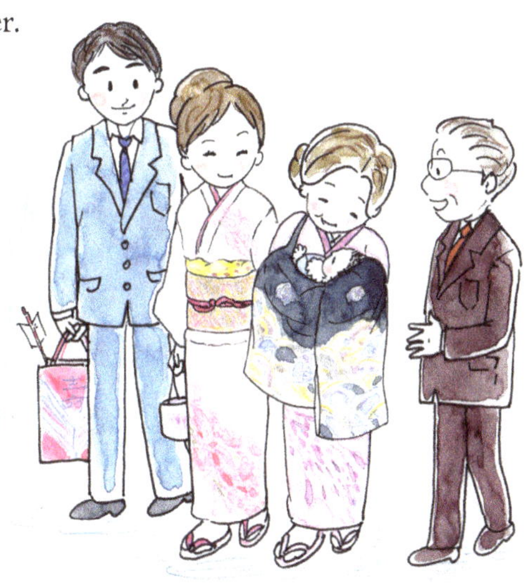

Example 2: Traditional Japanese Ceremony for Children

In Japan, there is an annual traditional ceremony for children who have or will become three, five, or seven years old in that year. The official date for the ceremony is November 15, but rituals can be held anytime from October to November and are popular on sunny weekends. Children of these ages are taken to a shrine by the family to pray for their healthy growth. There are some standards for wearing kimonos at this traditional Japanese ceremony.

- ◇ The mother usually wears a semiformal kimono. (P34, P50)
- ◇ The father usually wears a Western suit. (Reason: P16)

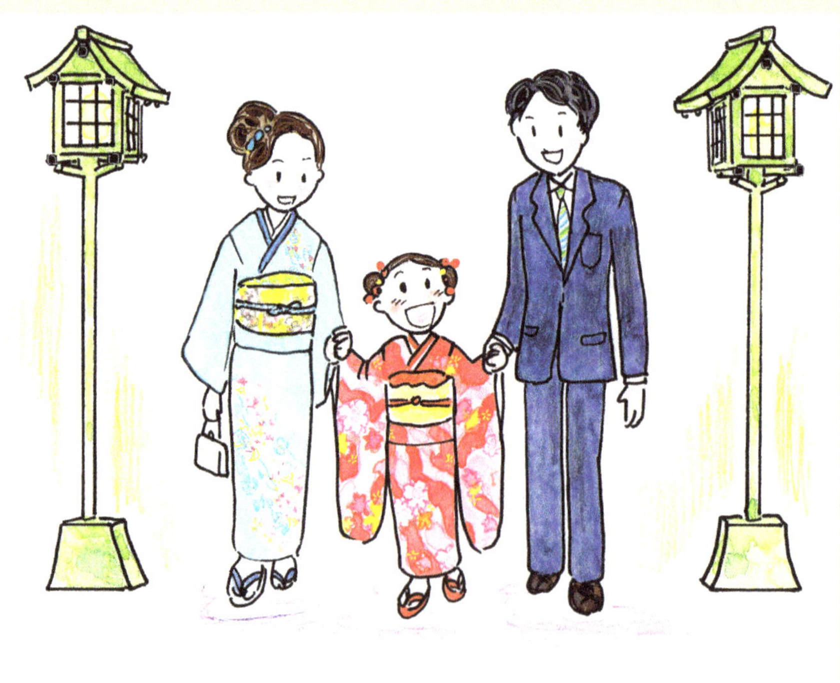

Shrines are places where Japanese people hold ceremonies.

Japanese-style wedding ceremonies and many other Japanese annual ceremonies are often held on Sundays at shrines. There are some temples and other venues to hold these ceremonies, too.

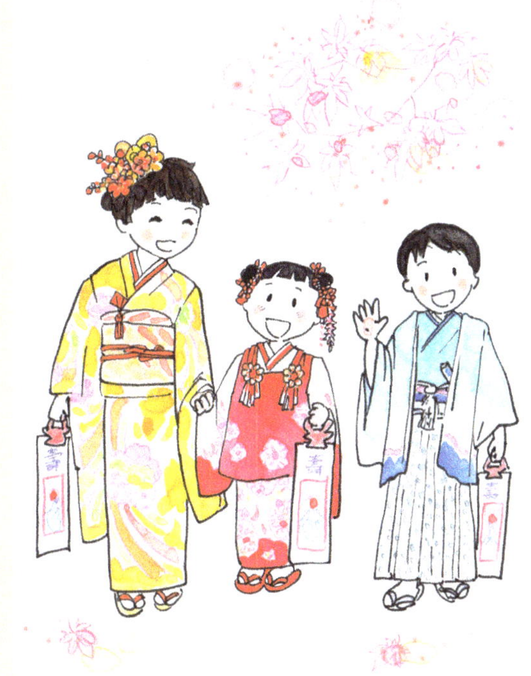

Seven-year-old girl's kimono   Five-year-old boy's kimono

Three-year-old girl's kimono

Access to Meiji shrine in Tokyo:

JR Yamanote Line Harajuku Station (JY19)

Subway Chiyoda Line Meijijingumae Station (C3)

Subway Fukutoshin Line Meijijingumae Station (F15)

6) *Iro-muji*: Traditional semiformal or informal kimonos for women

QUESTION 16

Is there a kimono equivalent to women's business suits?

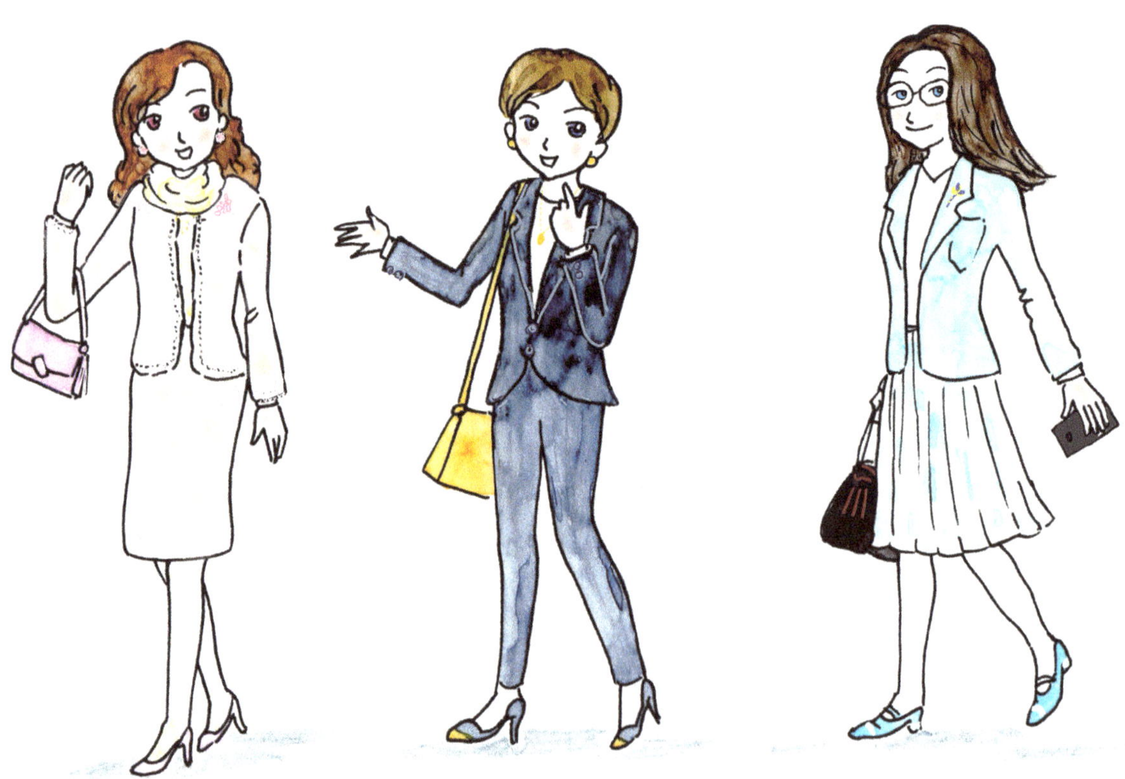

ANSWER 16

> *Iro-muji are simple and single-color kimonos. They are similar to women's business suits because they don't have any patterns and can be used for more serious occasions than other semiformal kimonos.*

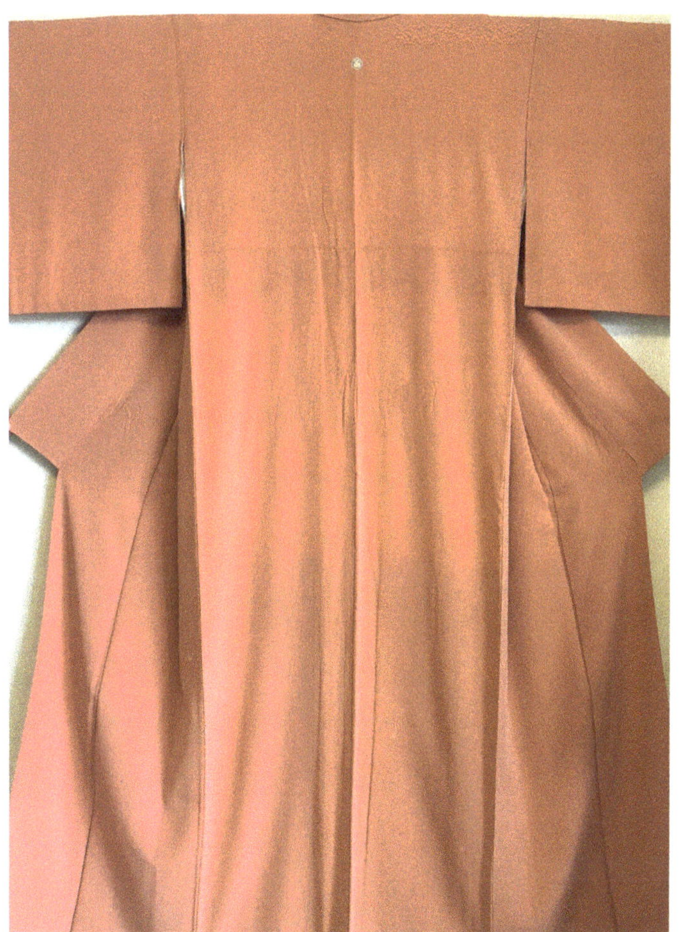

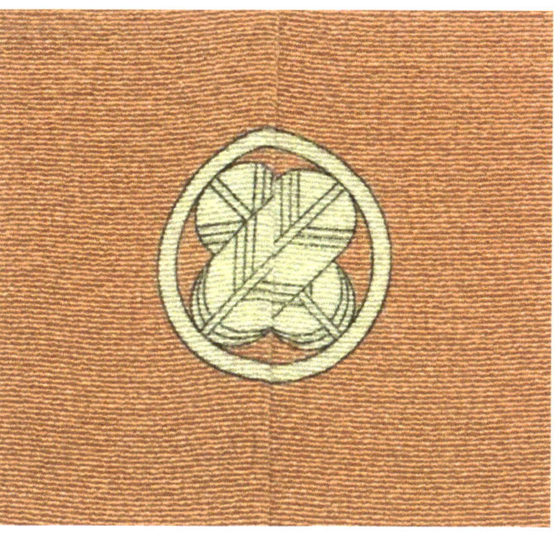

mon: family crest (P20)

Iro-muji: Traditional semiformal or informal kimonos for women

The rank of a kimono is established by the number of *mon*. If there are three *mon* or one *mon* on the kimono, it is regarded as a semiformal or informal kimono, respectively. If there are no *mon*, it is regarded as a casual kimono.

This kind of kimono most commonly has one *mon*, so they are suitable for attending various ceremonies and annual events in Japan.

Example 1: Traditional Japanese Tea Ceremony

When Japanese people participate in Japanese cultural activities such as the tea ceremony, they often wear kimonos. There are certain standards for wearing kimonos according to the occasion.

Iro-muji with one *mon* is a common style for many occasions.

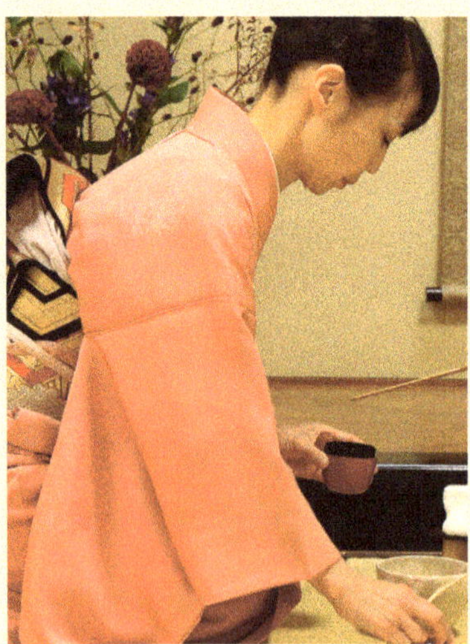

Tea ceremony

CHAPTER 4

Traditional Kimonos for Expressing the Seasons

Japanese people learn color coordination from nature.

Over the ages, kimono standards of dress have changed.

However, the basic patterns and unique Japanese color coordination that are considered "auspicious"—or *happy* and *ceremonial*—have been passed down from generation to generation.

In the Japanese kimono, color is mainly coordinated with nature, making the kimono more attractive and beautiful.

Slight changes in seasons are uniquely expressed in Japanese culture through various media, such as kimonos, poems, music, and art.

This chapter features seasonal images of Japanese kimonos, together with images of Japanese scenery and poems. *Haiku* is Japanese poetry consisting of seventeen syllables and always contain a seasonal word. In the Japanese language, there are millions of seasonal expressions. These feelings are alive also in the Japanese art of the kimono.

The suitable months and occasions mentioned in this chapter are examples based on the seasons in and around Tokyo.

1) *Komon*: Traditional informal kimonos for women

QUESTION 17

"*Is there a kimono equivalent to women's smart casual dresses?*"

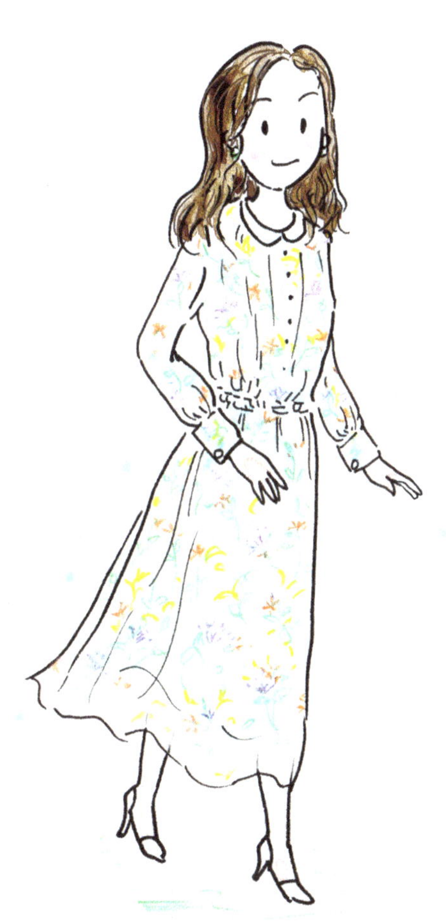

ANSWER 17

Fully patterned kimonos are usually regarded as informal kimonos, similar in purpose to Western smart casual attire. Japanese women will wear this type of kimono while they are enjoying the beauty of nature and the season.

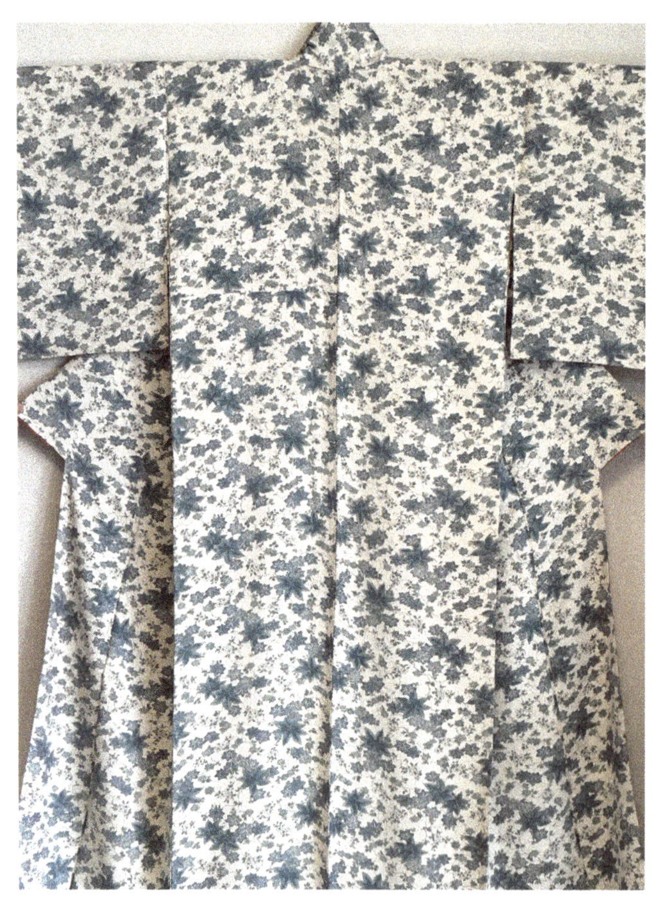

QUESTION 18

❝ Which season is suitable for the patterns and color coordination of this kimono? ❞

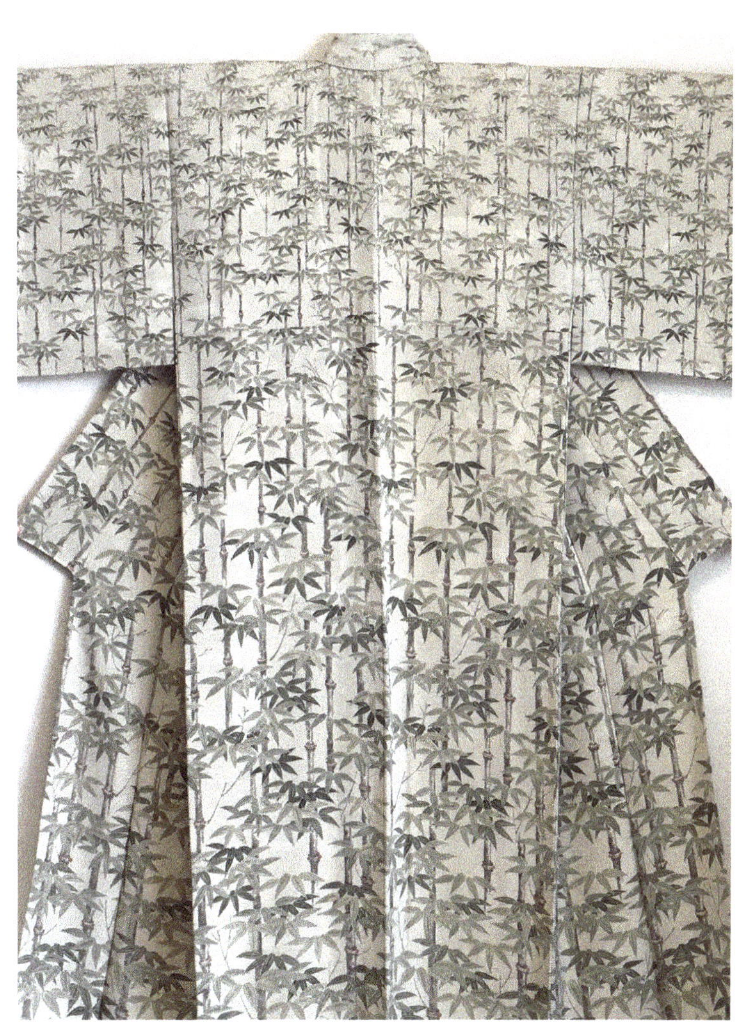

ANSWER 18

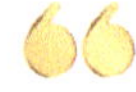 **New Year's Celebrations in January**

If the kimono has patterns that are considered "auspicious,"
it can be suitable for happy occasions such as
New Year's celebrations. 

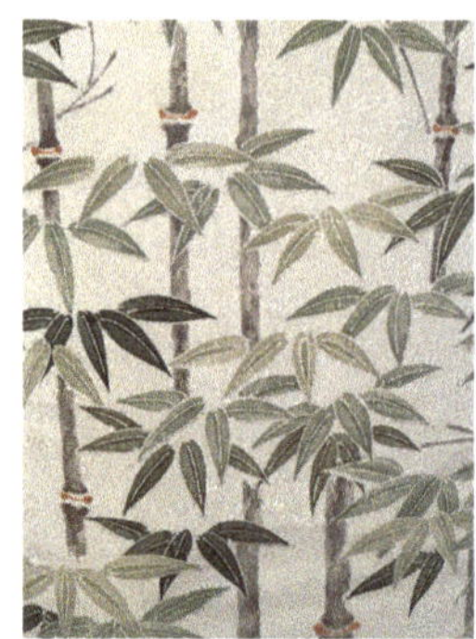

Japanese poem
"New Year's Sky"

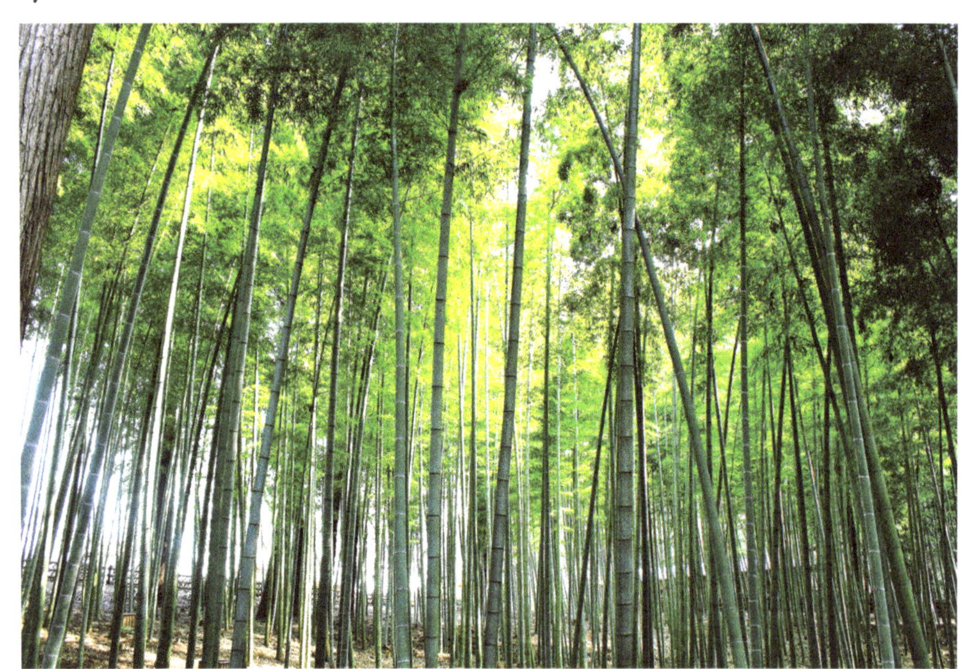

English meaning of this poem:

Above the bamboo forest/the New Year's sky/and our bright future emerge.

Japanese seasonal word: *hatsumisora* (New Year's sky)

QUESTION 19

Which season is suitable for the color coordination of this kimono?

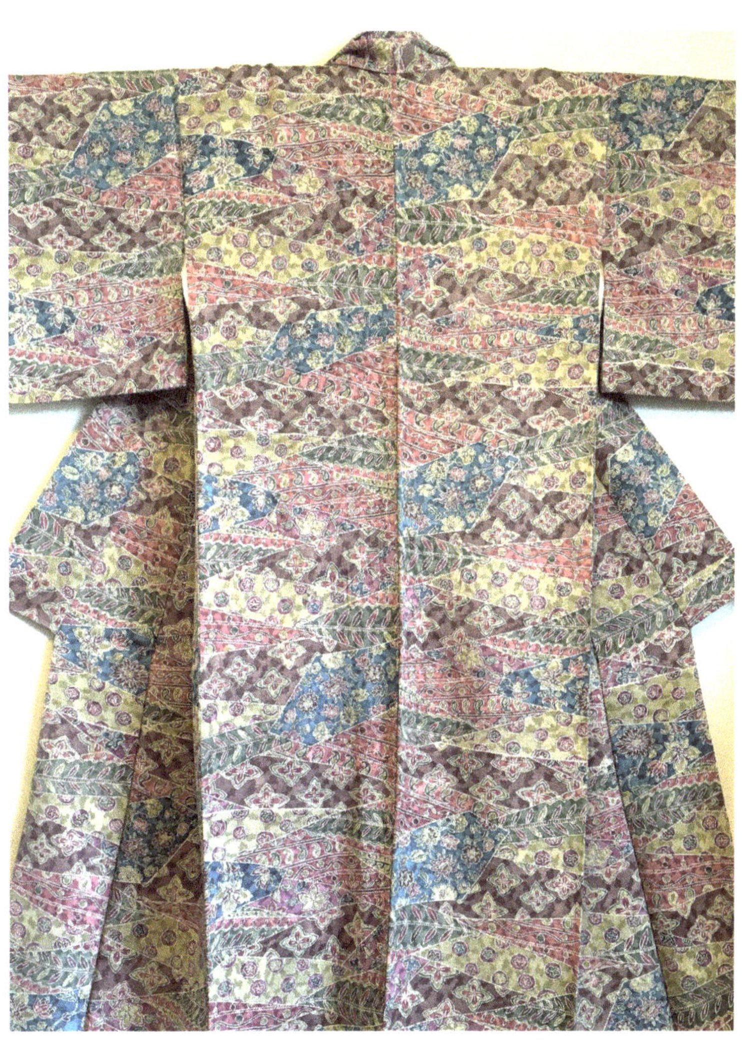

ANSWER 19

❝ *This color coordination can be seen in spring, specifically March and April.* ❞

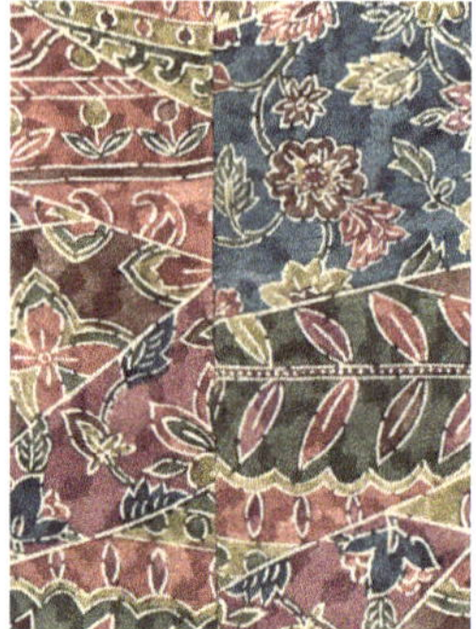

Japanese poem
"Spring Flowers"

菜の花の果ては断崖海の青

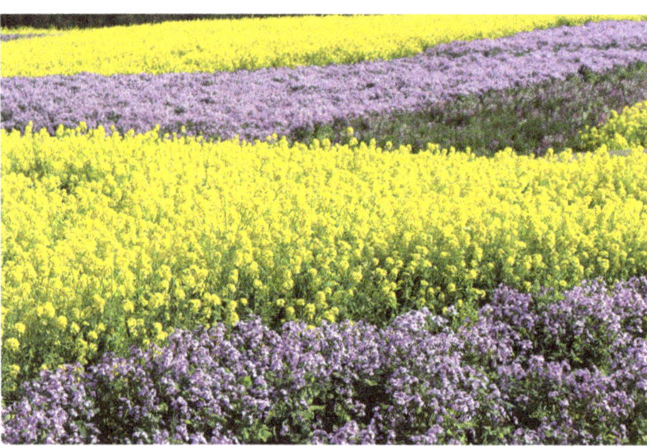

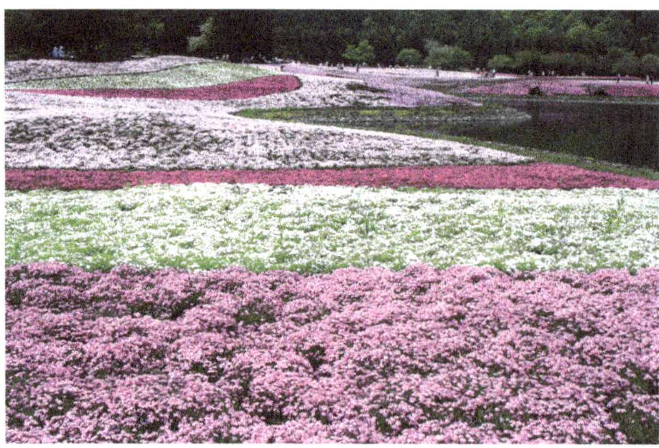

English meaning of the poem:

Above the spring-flower field/is the blue of the precipitous sea.

Japanese seasonal word: *nanohana* (spring flowers)

QUESTION 20

Which month is suitable for the patterns and color coordination of this kimono?

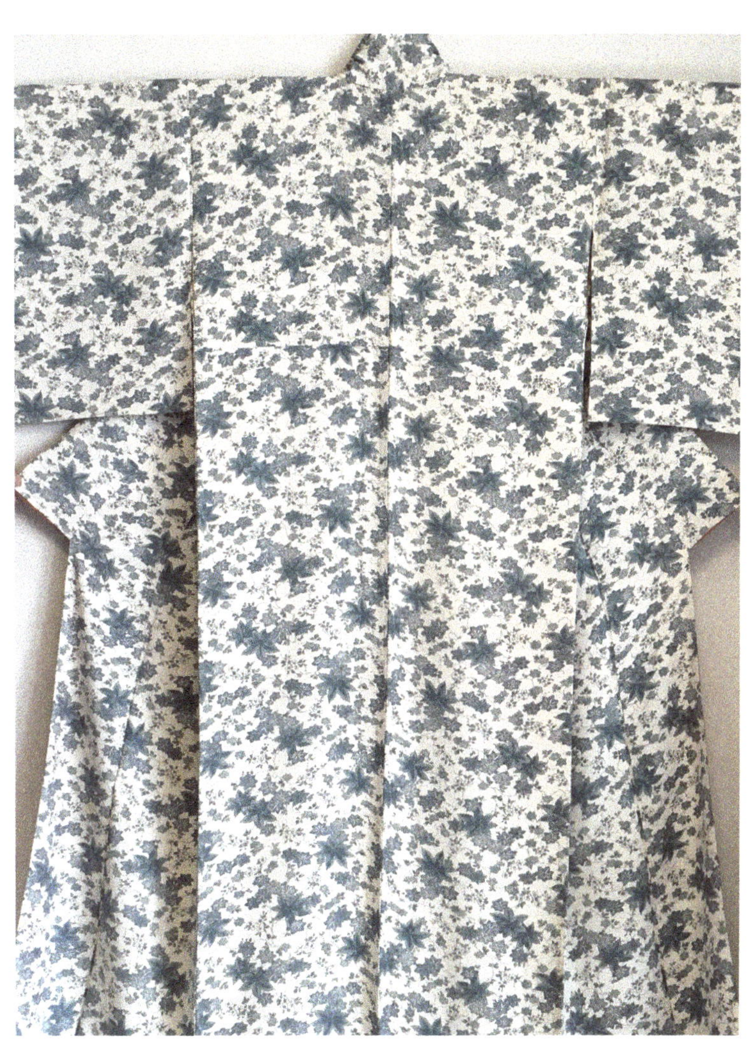

ANSWER 20

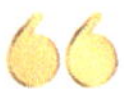 *The pattern of fresh green leaves is suitable for May.* 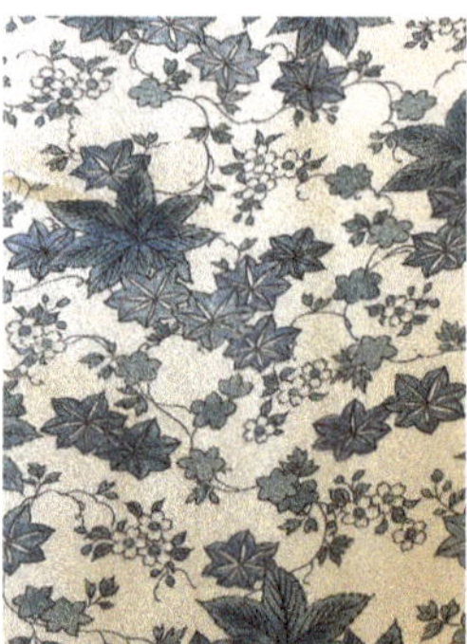

Japanese poem
"Fresh Green Leaves"

白雲を湖底に沈め若葉風

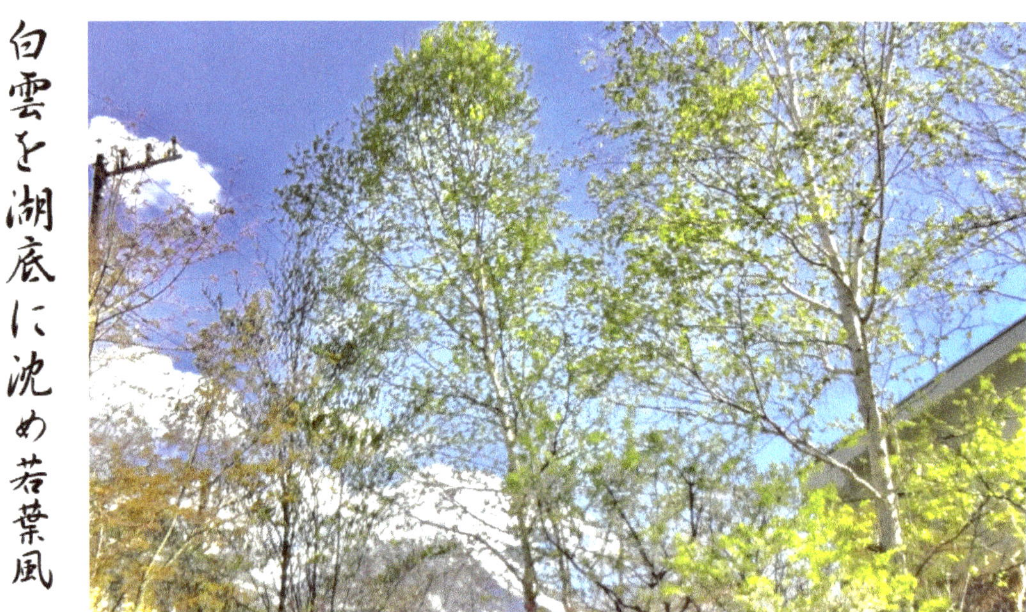

English meaning of the poem:

White clouds submerged/in the depths of the lake/a breeze/through the fresh green leaves.

Location: Lake Kawaguchi area in Yamanashi Prefecture

Japanese seasonal word: *wakaba* (fresh green leaves)

QUESTION 21

Which season is suitable for the patterns and color coordination of this kimono?

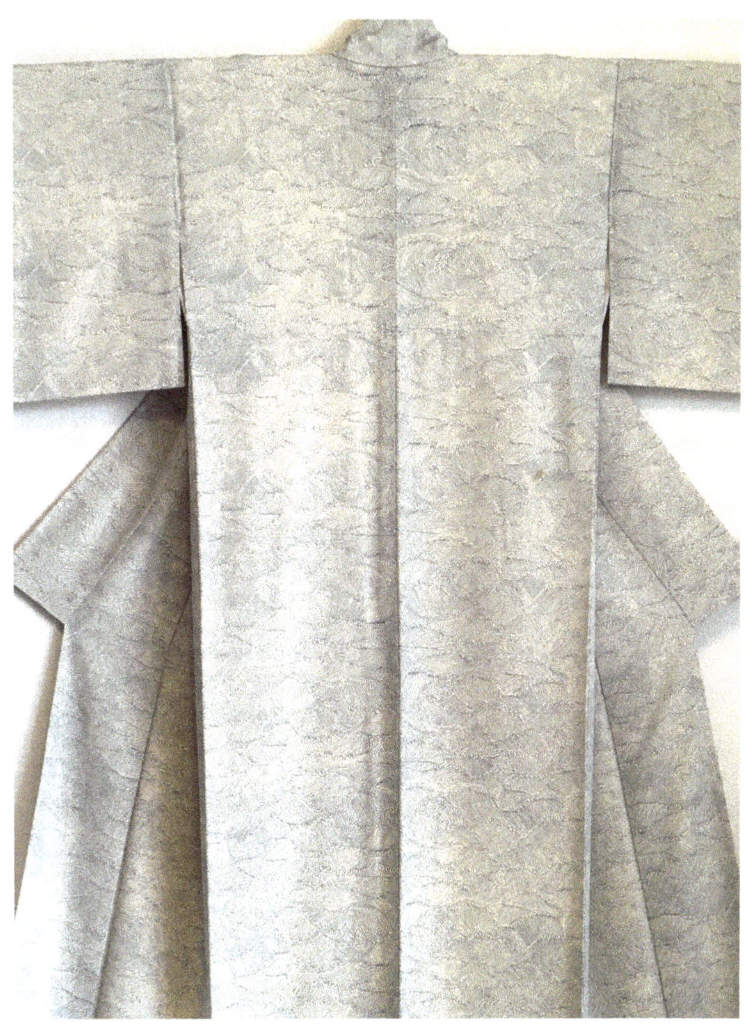

ANSWER 21

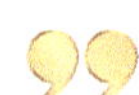 *Because of the pattern of great summer waves, this kimono is suitable for summer.* 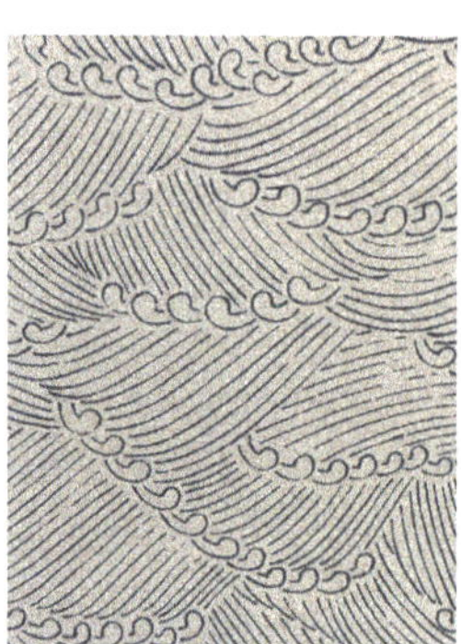

Japanese poem
"Great Summer Waves"

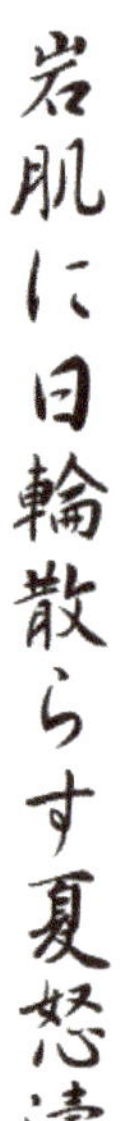
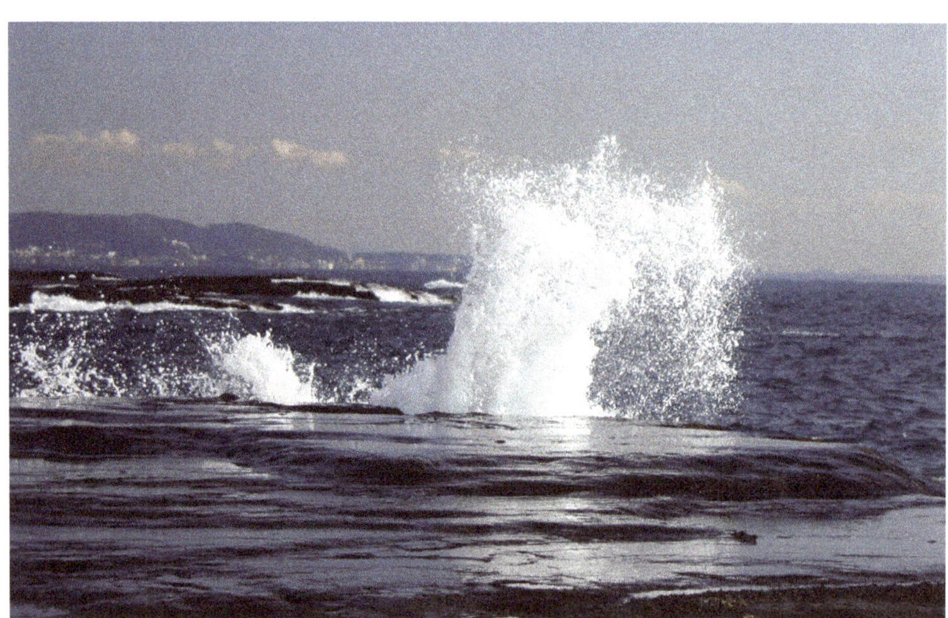

English meaning of the poem:

Great summer waves/scatter the sun/over the rock face.

Location: Enoshima Island in Kanagawa Prefecture

Japanese seasonal word: *natsudotou* (great summer waves)

64

QUESTION 22

❝ *Which month is suitable for the patterns and color coordination of this kimono?* ❞

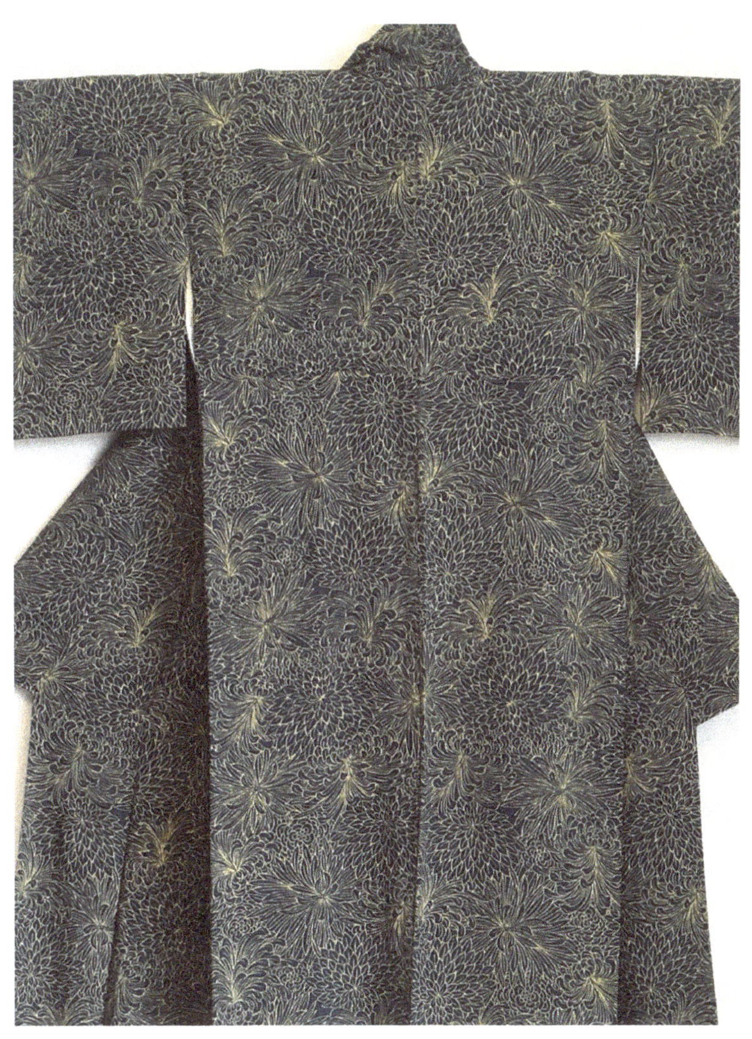

ANSWER 22

> 66 **This kimono is suitable for October, because chrysanthemum flowers bloom beautifully at this time.** 99

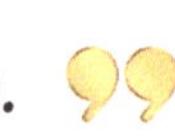

Japanese poem
"Chrysanthemums"

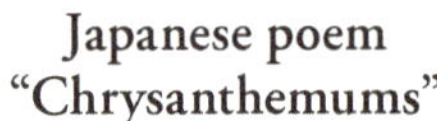

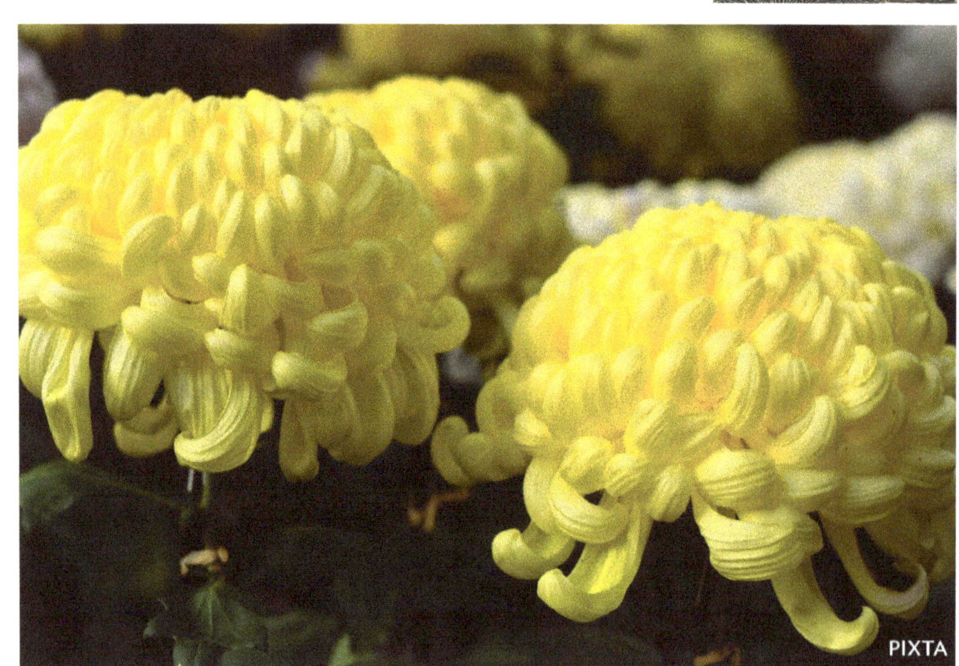

English meaning of the poem:

Chrysanthemum petals/layer into/a beautiful deep yellow

Japanese seasonal word: *kikukahen* (petals of chrysanthemums)

QUESTION 23

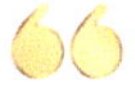 *Which month is suitable for the patterns and color coordination of this kimono?*

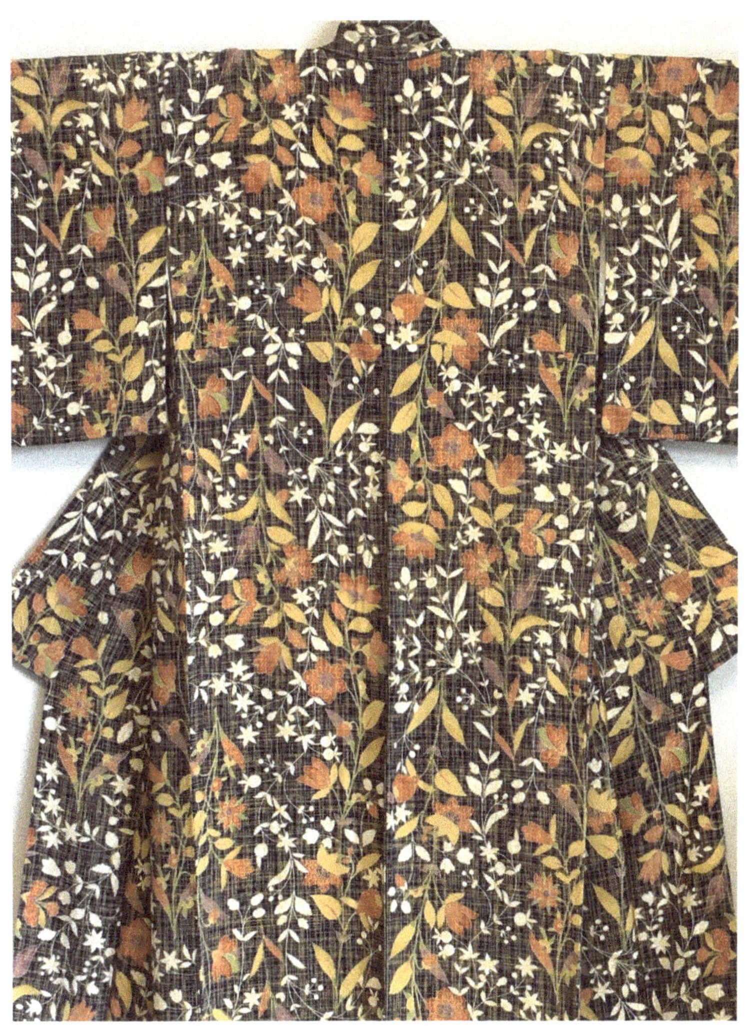

ANSWER 23

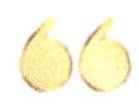 **This kimono is suitable for November because of the beautifully colored mountain leaves.**

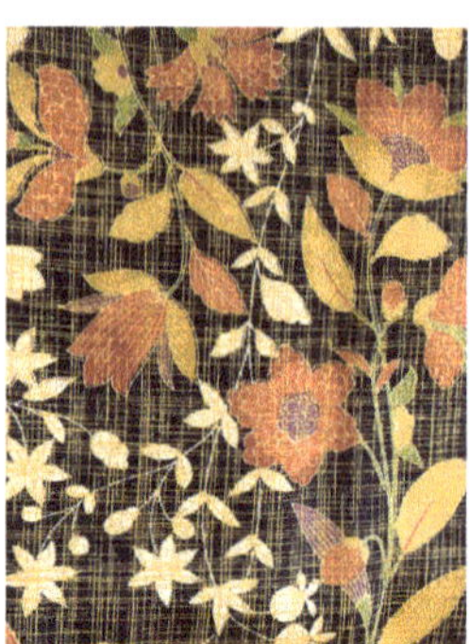

Japanese poem
"Winter Maple Trees"

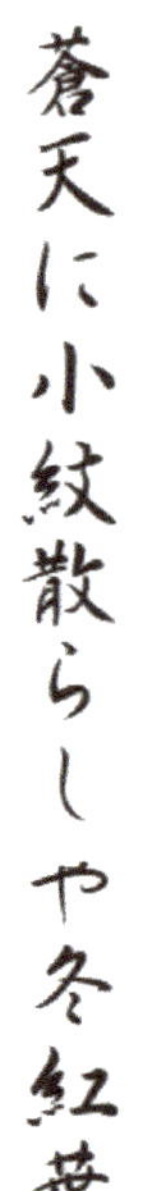

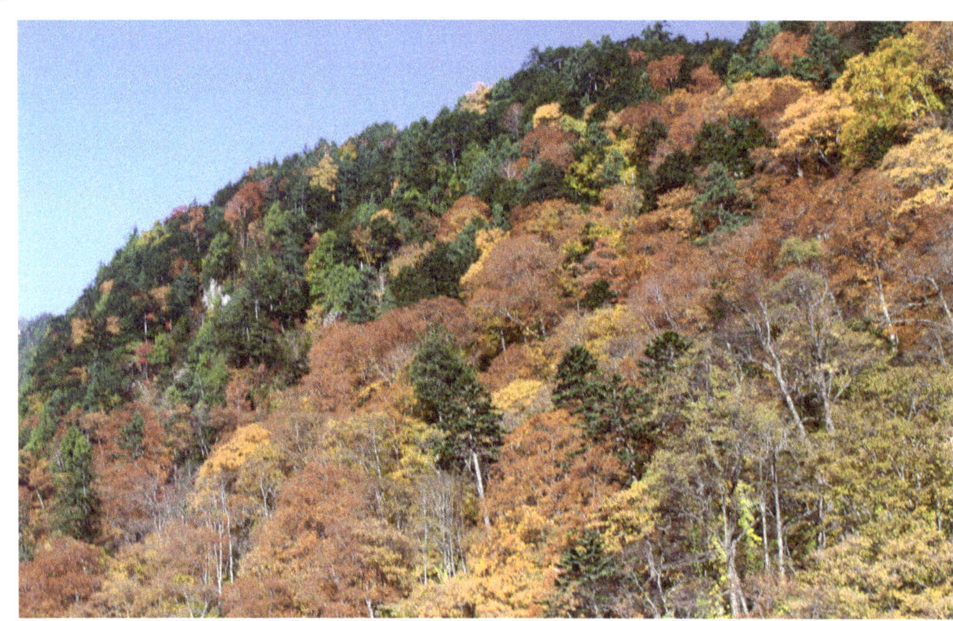

English meaning of the poem:

Beautifully colored leaves/are scattered/across the azure sky

Japanese seasonal word: *fuyumomiji* (winter maple trees)

Materials for Traditional Kimonos

QUESTION 24

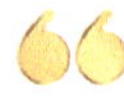 *What materials are traditional kimonos made from?*

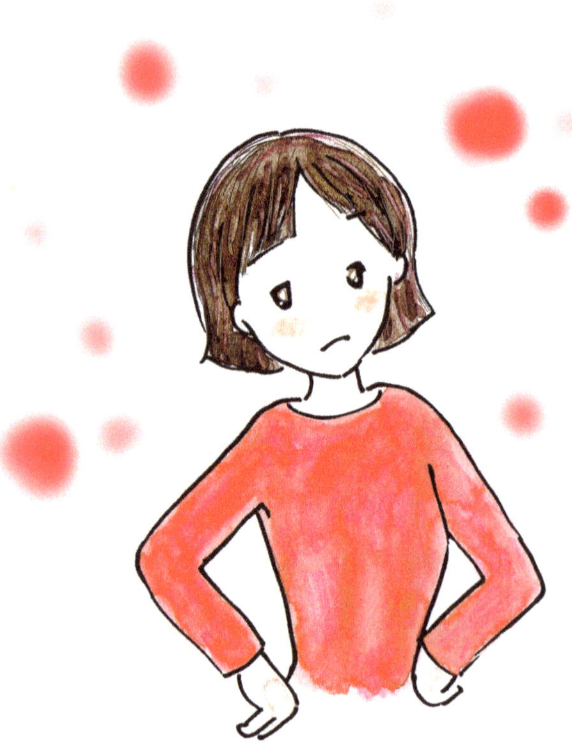

ANSWER 24

There are mainly two different kinds of silk used to make traditional kimonos.

1. Ki-ito—A silk thread which is made by reeling silk thread from cocoons.

This kind of silk is usually used for making formal kimonos, semiformal kimonos, and informal kimonos. Many traditional kimonos (explained from Chapter 2 to Chapter 4 in this book) utilize this silk thread as a material.

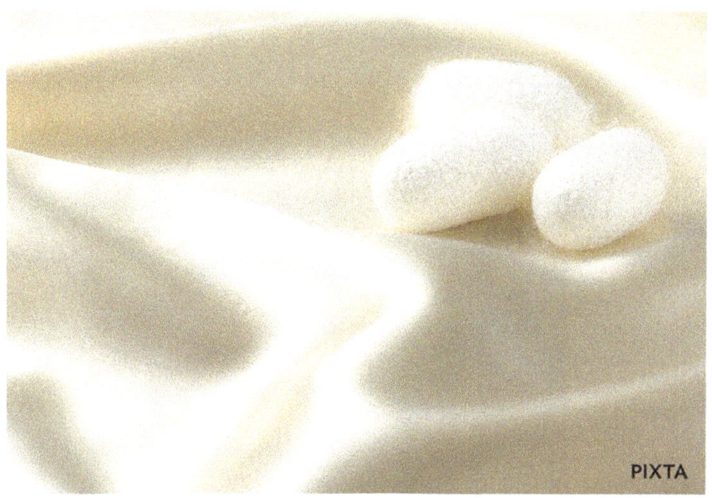

2. Tsumugi-ito—A silk thread made by making a floss from cocoons and then making yarn from the floss by spinning.

This thread is called tsumugi-ito and is used to make kimonos called tsumugi kimonos. It is a unique Japanese handicraft. Tsumugi-ito silk thread is never used for formal kimonos—only for casual kimonos. Still, tsumugi kimonos are sometimes expensive.

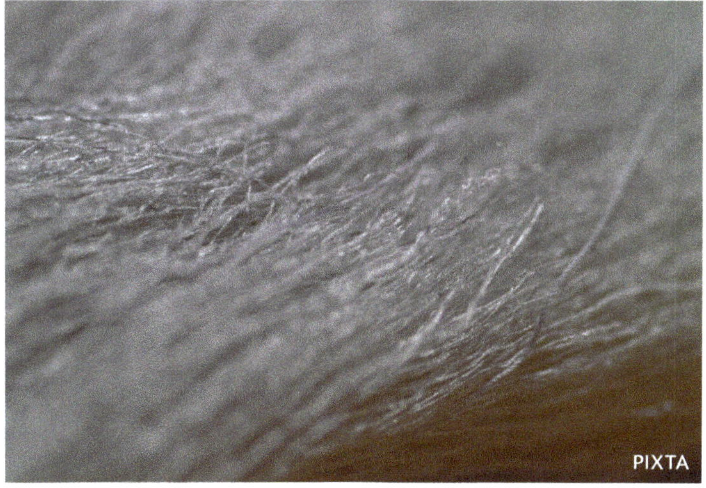

1) *Tsumugi*: Traditional casual kimonos

Tsumugi is a type of kimono made from *tsumugi-ito* silk thread, using specific traditional Japanese weaving techniques. The textured surface of the kimono differs according to the area of production.

This is a casual kimono, but it can still be very expensive. One example of a high-quality specialty *tsumugi* kimono from Ibaraki Prefecture is Yuki-*tsumugi*.

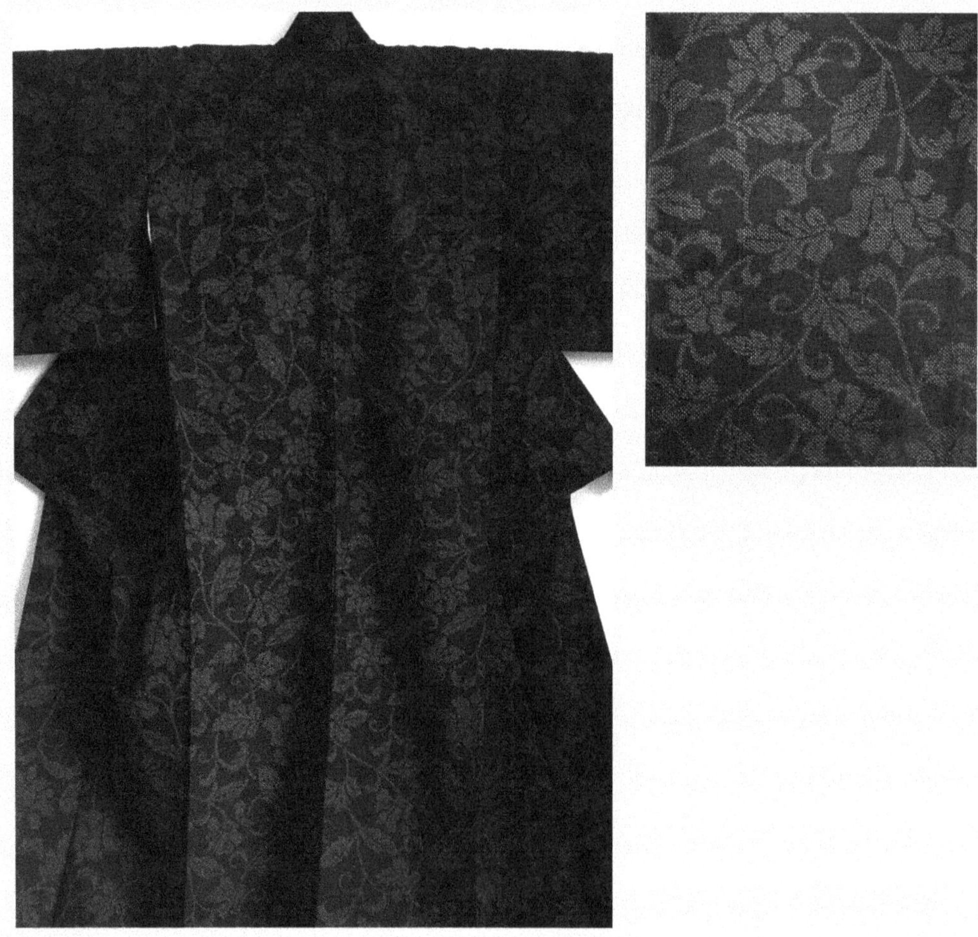

Yuki-*tsumugi*

2) *Momen*: Traditional casual kimonos

QUESTION 25

66 What materials are used for traditional kimonos other than silk? 99

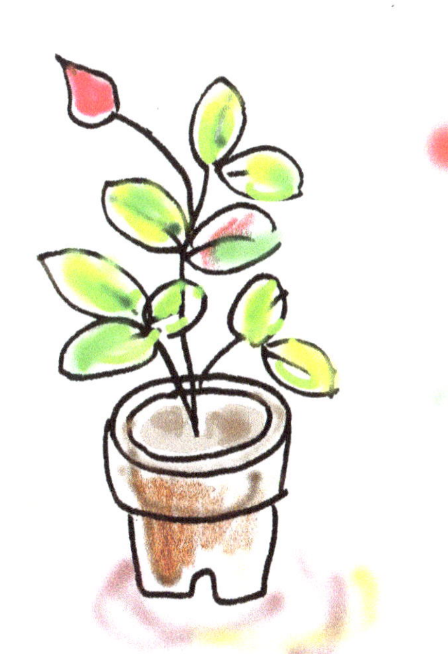

ANSWER 25

66 *Cotton is another essential material used*
for traditional casual kimonos.
*Cotton thread is called **momen-ito**, so kimonos*
*made with this thread are called **momen** kimonos.* 99

Cotton *(momen)*

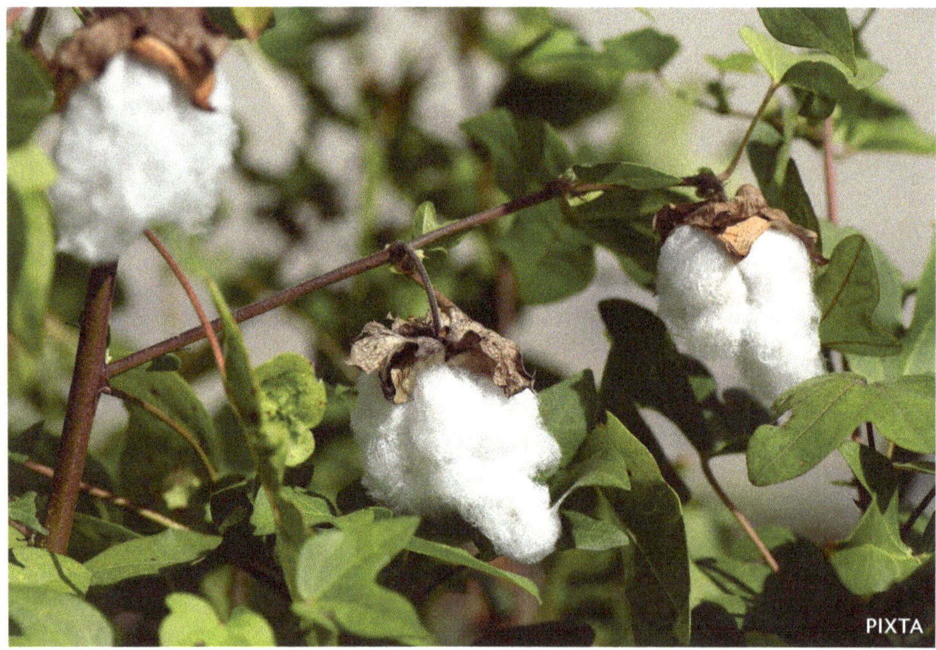

Cotton threads are made from raw cotton, which comes from the seeds of tall plants.
Cotton can be made into yarn by being spun. Cloth made of cotton has a nice texture and good water absorbency. It is a commonly used material for clothes all over the world.

Momen: Traditional casual kimonos

Momen is the Japanese word for "cotton." It also refers to a type of everyday cotton kimono.

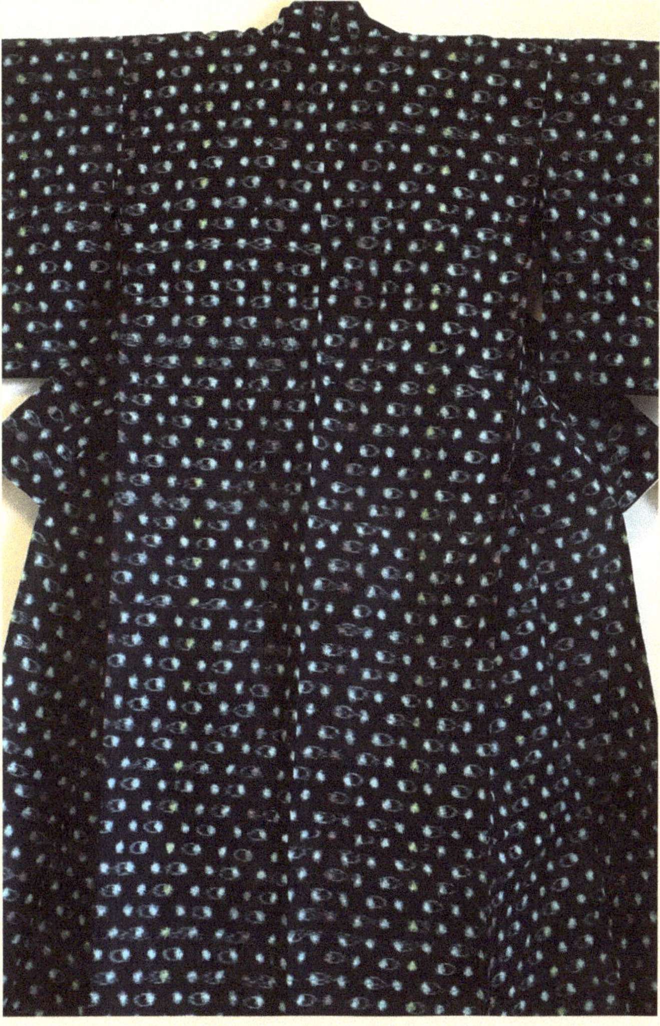

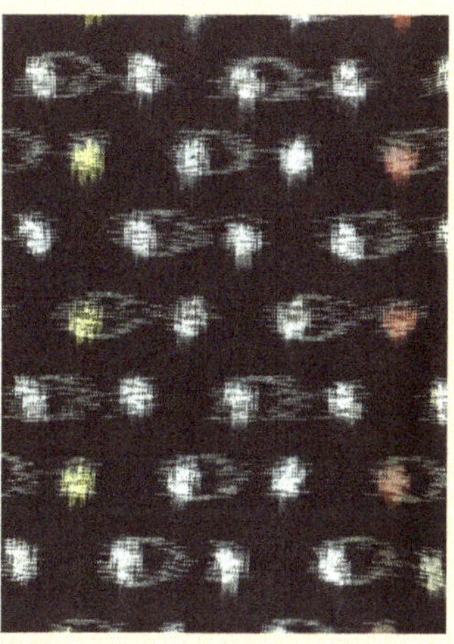

This is a *momen* kimono.

QUESTION 26

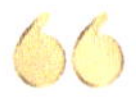 *What is the difference between* **momen** *kimonos and* **yukata**? 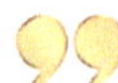

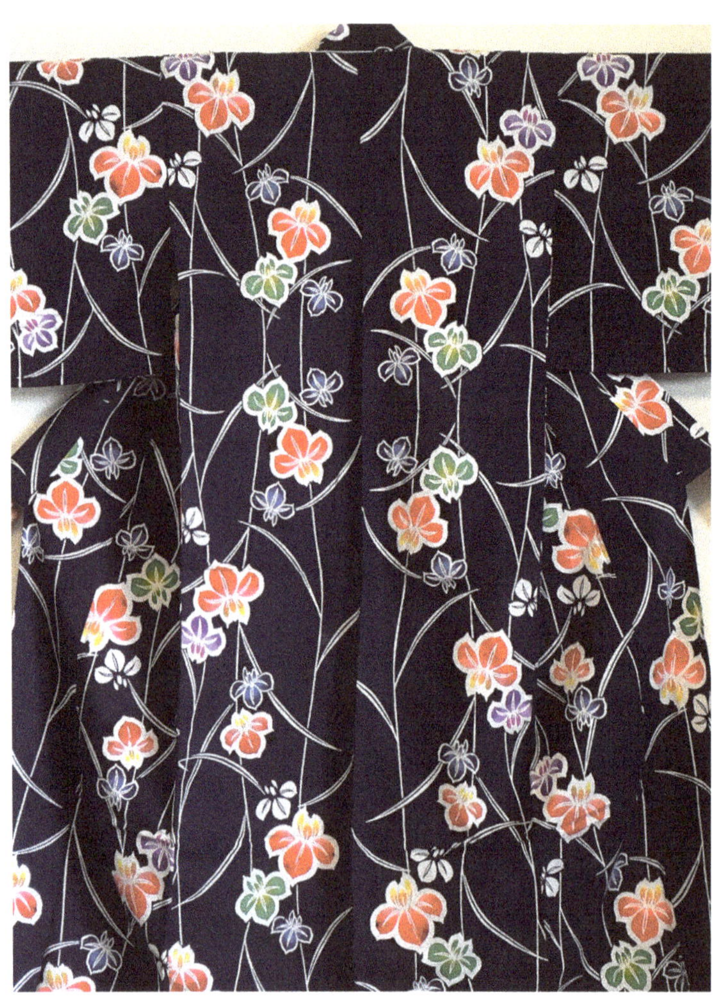

This is a *yukata*.

ANSWER 26

The main difference between *momen* kimonos and *yukata* is the collars. *Momen* kimonos need underwear to have double collars, and *yukata* have a single collar.

Another difference is the process used to make them.

Cotton kimonos are commonly made by weaving dyed threads.

On the other hand, to make *yukata*, white cotton cloth is first made and then dyed with the patterns. They typically have summer images, as *yukata* are worn during the summer.

**Japanese poem
"Fireworks Display"**

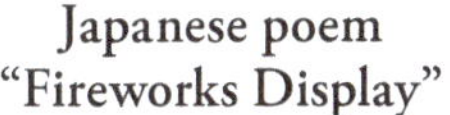

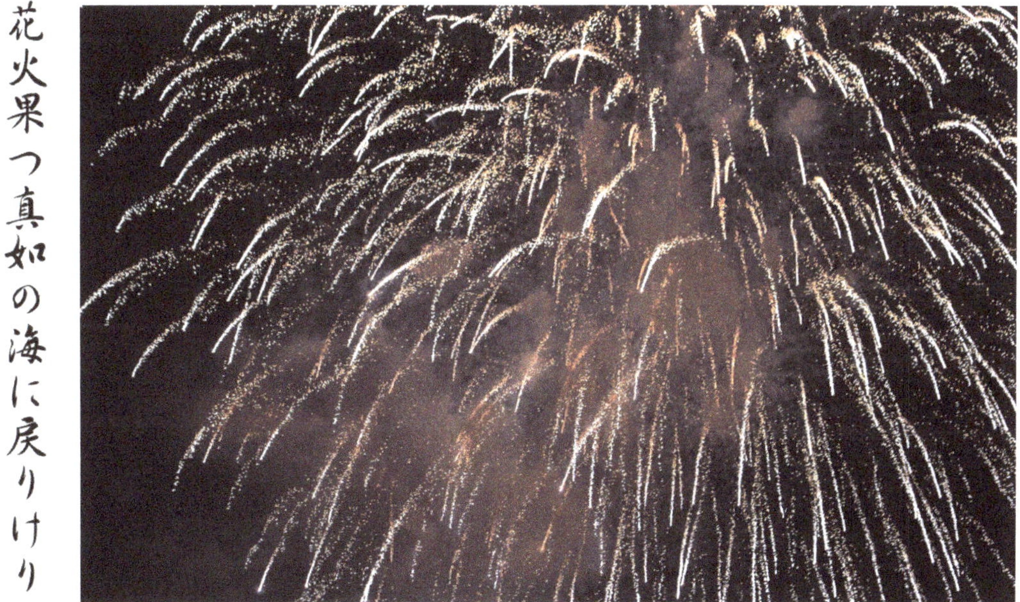

English meaning of the poem:

After a lively fireworks display/the sea returns suddenly/to silence.

Japanese seasonal word: *hanabi* (a fireworks display)

CHAPTER 6

Traditional Obi Sashes and Kimono Accessories

1) Traditional *obi* sashes

A jacket can be used to "dress up" or "dress down" Western clothes. How can this be done with kimonos?

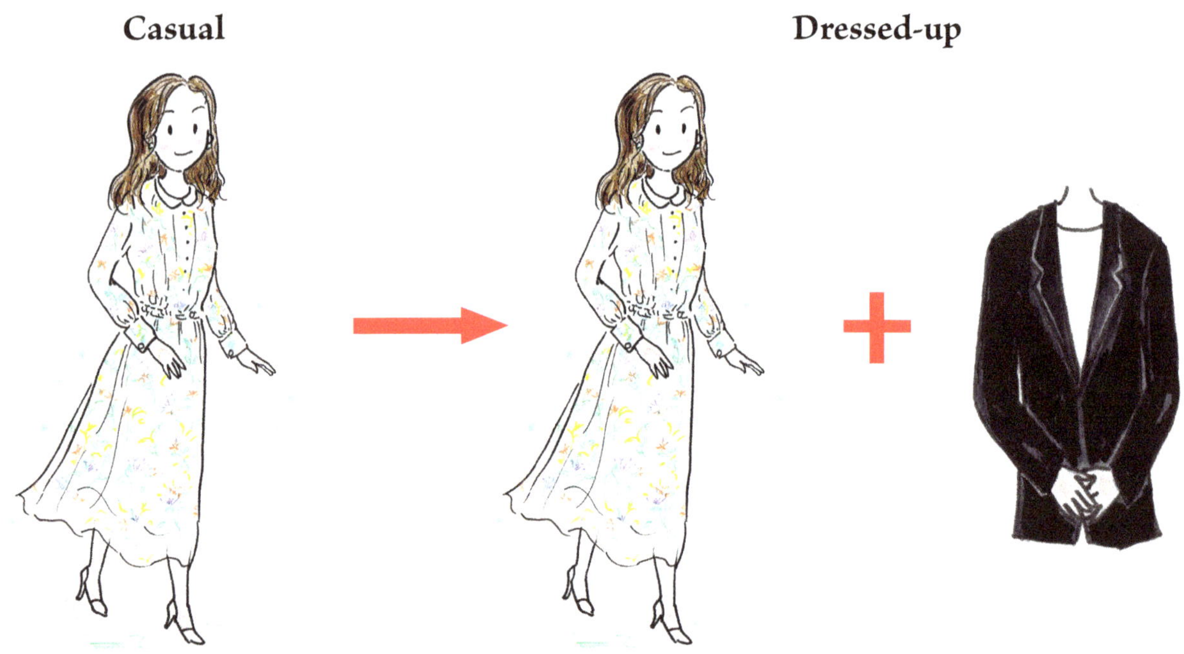

ANSWER 27

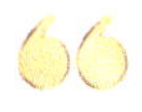 *An **obi** sash can change the rank of a kimono, in much the same way that a jacket can be used for Western clothes.*

For Western clothes, if a suit jacket is worn over a casual dress, it makes the attire more formal.

A denim jacket can be worn over an informal dress to make the attire more casual.

In this case, a suitable jacket or blazer may be chosen to match the occasion.

An *obi* sash for a kimono works like the Western jacket, so it is vital to choose an *obi* sash suitable to the kimono and the occasion. An *obi* sash with a kimono can result in a beautiful coordination.

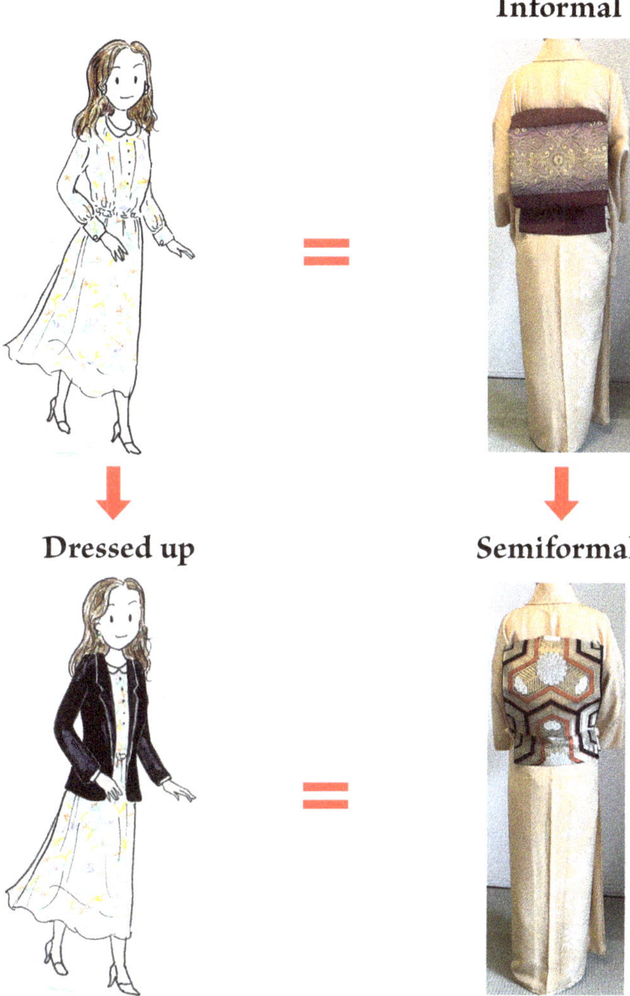

Classifications of traditional *obi* sashes

In ancient times, braided ropes were used to tie kimonos. *Obi* sashes later developed into their current style. *Obi* sashes became wider, longer, and more beautiful, due to the development of traditional Japanese weaving and dyeing techniques.

Obi sashes can be roughly classified into eight groups, according to their size and the technique used to make them. Because *obi* sashes can change the rank of the kimono, choosing an *obi* sash suitable to the occasion is vital.

1. *Maruobi* : A gorgeous *obi* sash for women

Maruobi is the most exquisite type of *obi* sash. Because of the elaborate designs, a *maruobi* sash is much heavier than other types of *obi* sashes. It is made of a patterned silk cloth, 436 centimeters in length. It is about 35 centimeters in width, and both the outer side and inner side can bear the same gorgeous design. This style of *obi* sash began to be made around the 18th century after skillfully woven cloth was imported from China. However, kimono styles became simpler after the middle of the 20th century, and *maruobi* became less common. Today, it is used mainly for wedding kimonos (P10) and *maiko* kimonos (P13).

2. *Fukuroobi*: Formal *obi* sash for women

Fukuroobi is an *obi* sash of about 31 centimeters in width and more than 420 centimeters in length. The front side is beautifully decorated with auspicious patterns made by traditional weaving and dyeing techniques. The back side is usually a simple silk cloth without designs. *Fukuroobi* sashes and *maruobi* sashes are significantly different. *Fukuroobi* sashes date from around the latter 19th century, after *maruobi* sashes became less popular. Then, the *fukuroobi* sash replaced the *maruobi* sash as the most suitable *obi* sash for formal ceremonies. Today, most *fukuroobi* sashes are made with gold-and-silver auspicious patterns.

However, there are some *fukuroobi* sashes featuring simple patterns without gold-and-silver colors. These *fukuroobi* sashes are called *shareobi* and are less formal than the gold-and-silver ones.

Fukuroobi:

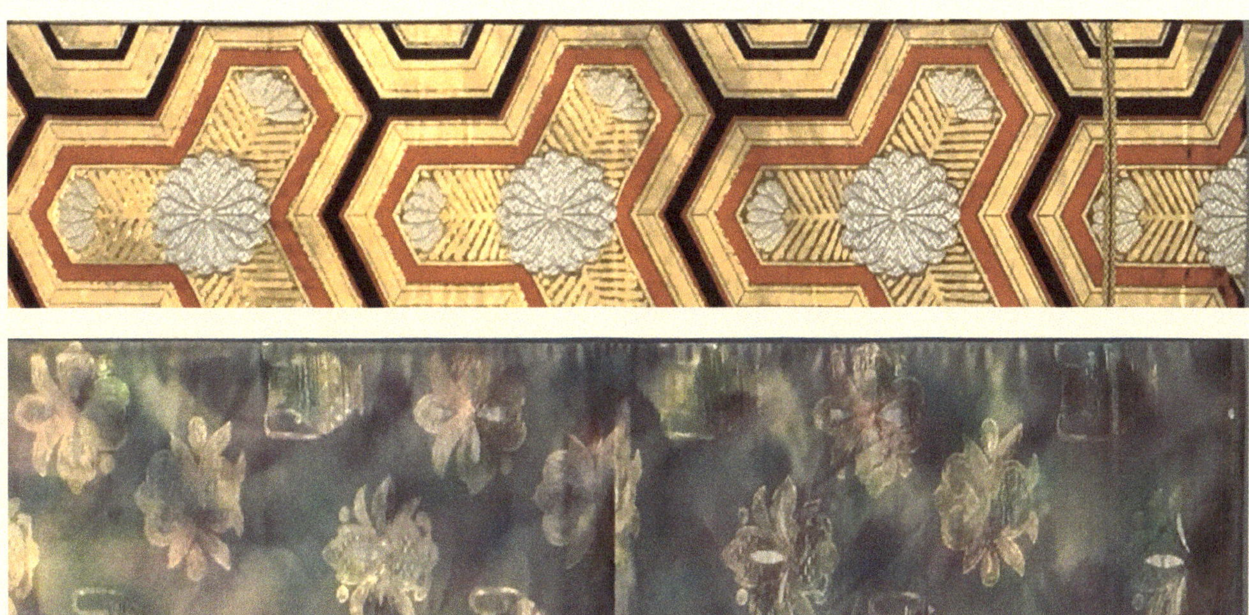

3. *Nagoyaobi:* An informal *obi* sash for women

A *nagoyaobi* sash is about 30 centimeters in width and about 360 centimeters in length. It is much shorter and lighter than formal *obi* sashes, so it is easy to tie. *Nagoyaobi* sashes with gold-and-silver auspicious patterns can be worn on semiformal occasions, but they are more typically seen on informal and casual occasions.

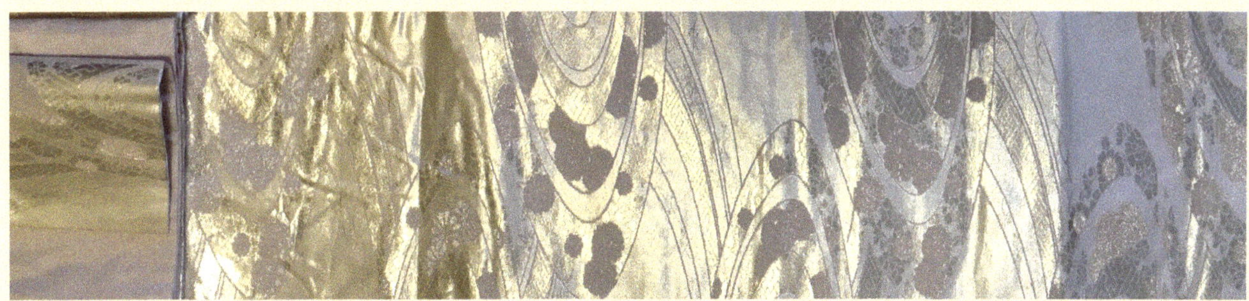

4. *Fukuro-nagoyaobi:* An informal *obi* sash for women

A *fukuro-nagoyaobi* sash is a single-layer, woven *obi* sash that was created in the mid-20th century to combine the concepts of the *fukuroobi* sash (P82) and the *nagoyaobi* sash (P83). It usually is worn on informal occasions and casual occasions.

Today, it is not very commonly used.

5. *Kyo-fukuroobi* : An informal *obi* sash for women

A *kyo-fukuroobi* is an *obi* sash that has the same shape as a *fukuroobi* sash (P82) and the same size as a *nagoyaobi* sash (P83). It is less formal than *fukuroobi* sashes and more formal than *nagoyaobi* sashes.

Today, it is not very common.

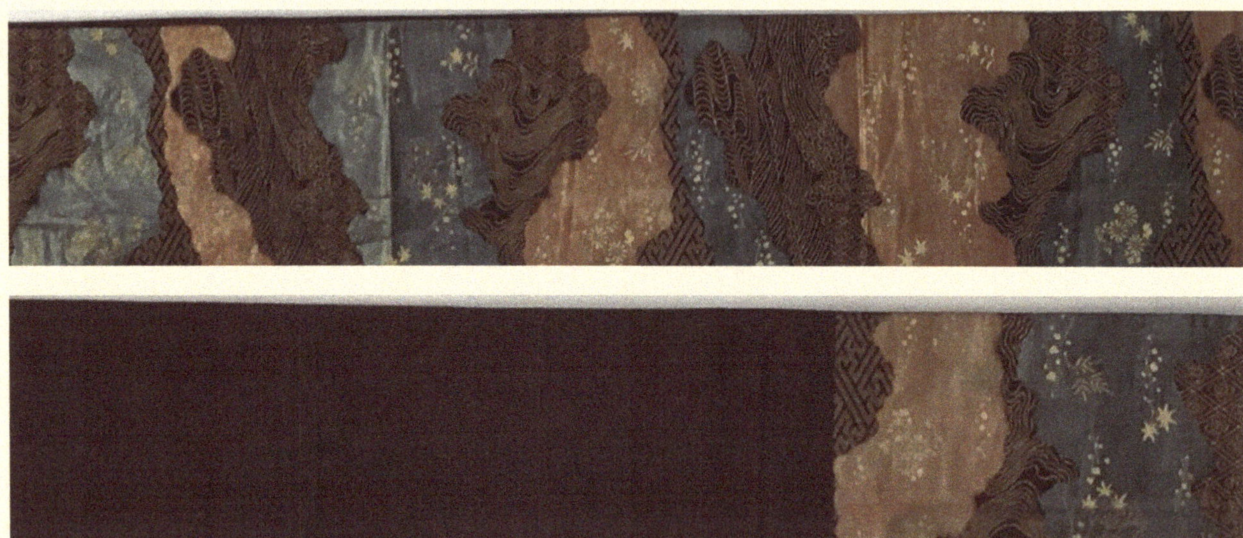

6. *Hosoobi/Hanhabaobi* : a narrow casual *obi* sash for women

Hosoobi sashes—or *hanhabaobi* sashes—are narrow casual *obi* sashes. Some of them are made of high-quality silk and can be suitable for a child's formal kimono.

Many of them are used in casual kimonos (Chapter 1).

7. *Kakuobi:* An *obi* sash mainly for men

Kakuobi is an *obi* sash for men. It is about 10 centimeters in width and about 4 meters in length. When a *kakuobi* is chosen, it is essential to select suitable materials for the occasion.

8. *Hekoobi:* A soft casual *obi* sash for everyone.

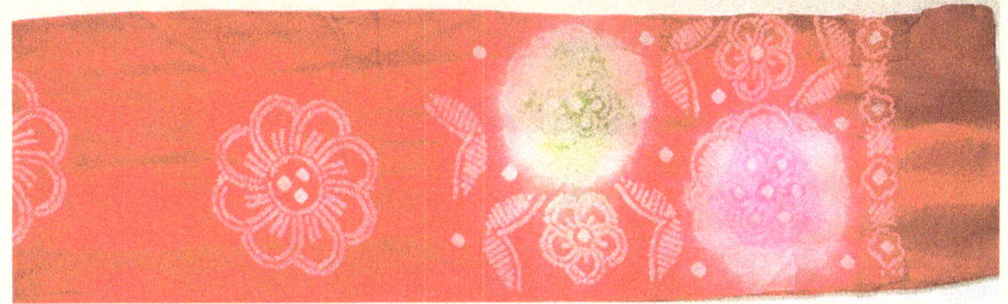

Haori: Jackets and Cardigans

QUESTION 28

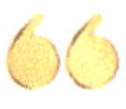 *What is the kimono equivalent to cardigans?* 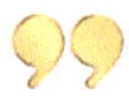

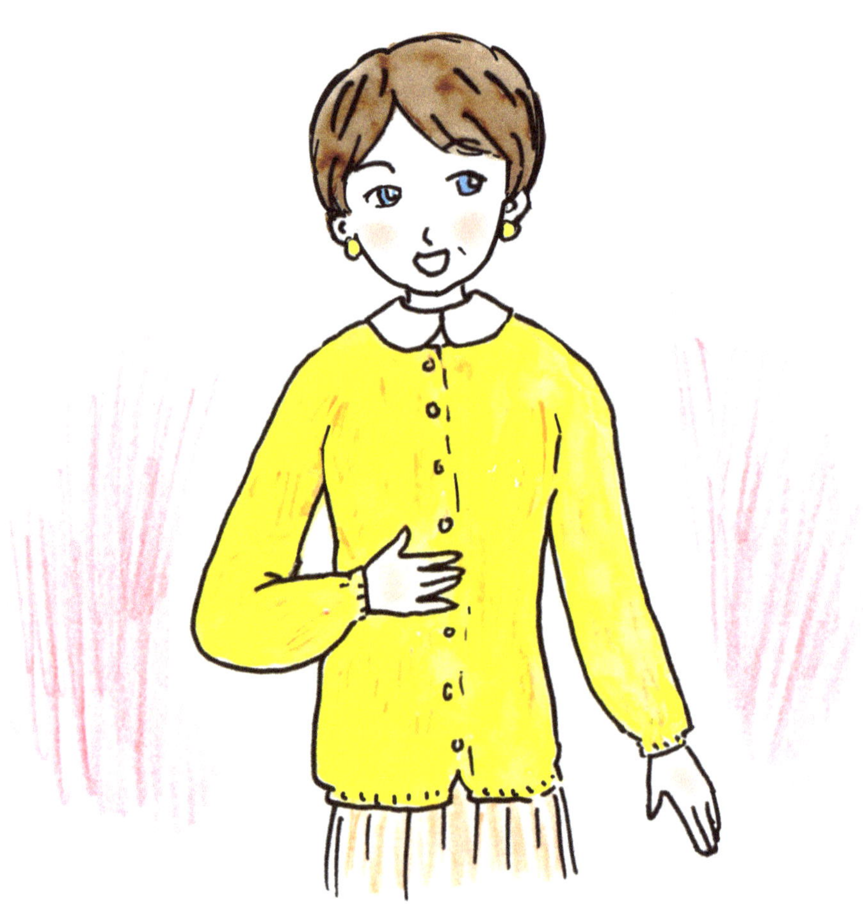

ANSWER 28

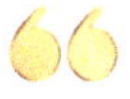 ***Haori** are like casual cardigans for women's kimonos.* 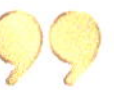

They are short and comfortable to wear. *Haori* serve different purposes for men and women.

For women's kimonos, they are the equivalent to casual cardigans.

For men's kimonos, they are the equivalent to formal suit jackets (P17).

They are popular souvenirs for tourists.

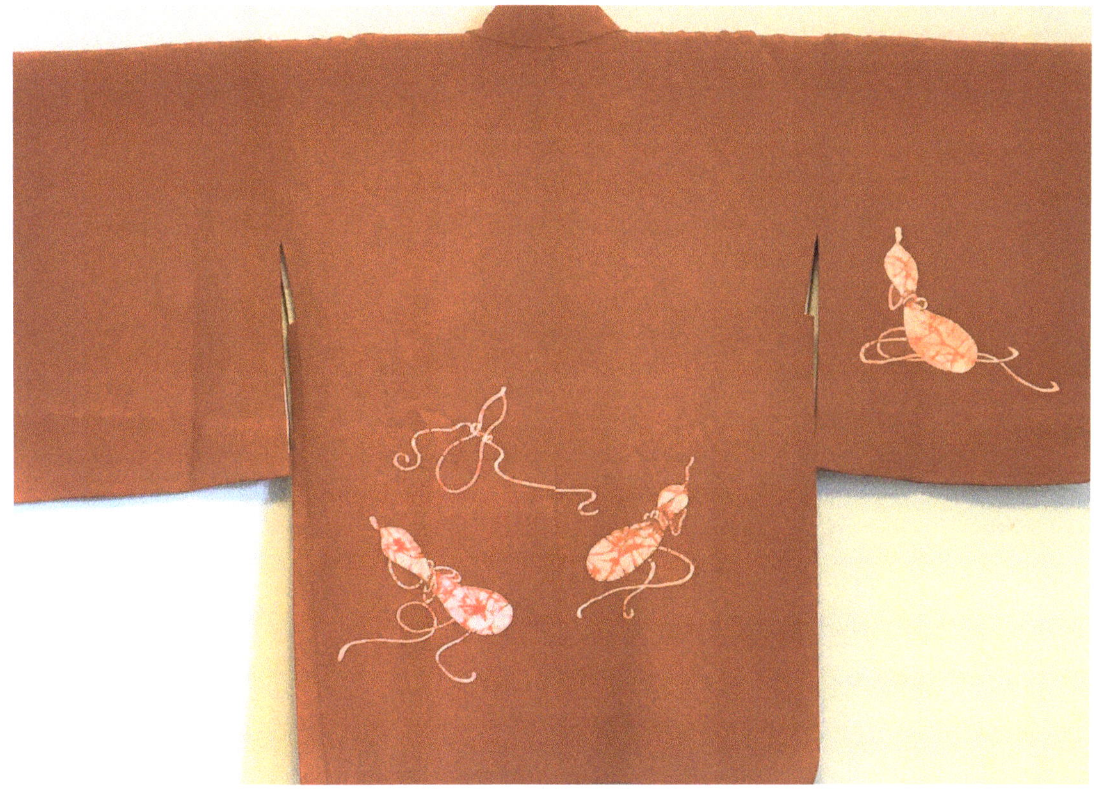

Haori for women

3) *Nagajuban*: Underwear

QUESTION 29

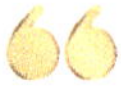 *What is underwear like for kimonos?* 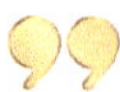

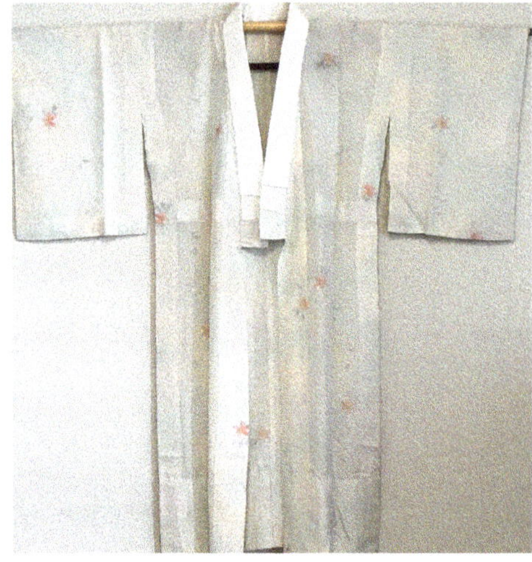

For women

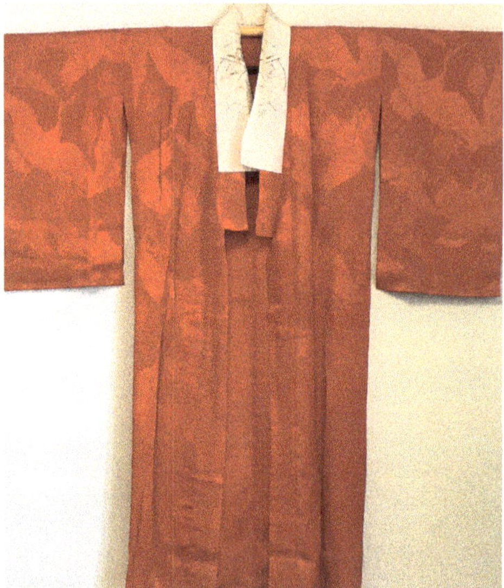

For children

ANSWER 29

Nagajuban is underwear for kimonos.

It is worn under the kimono to make a double-layered collar.

Although it is underwear, recently overseas tourists have been buying this underwear to use as loungewear.

Traditional *nagajuban* underwear is often made of beautiful silk and has a shorter length than a regular kimono. Children's *nagajuban* have pleats at the shoulders that are often more colorful than those for adults.

4) Kimono accessories

QUESTION 30

" What kind of kimono accessories can you recommend for tourists who want to purchase a souvenir? "

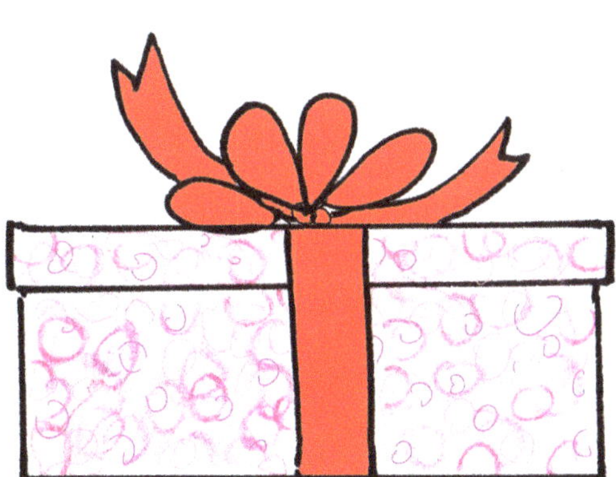

ANSWER 30

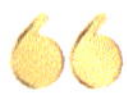 *Wrapping cloths with beautiful patterns, called **furoshiki**, and Japanese paper napkins used during Japanese tea ceremony, called **kaishi**, are recommended as souvenirs.*

Kaishi

Furoshiki

Furoshiki: **Wrapping cloth with beautiful patterns**

Furoshiki is a simple square cloth used for wrapping. It can be folded into various shapes and can even be folded into a lovely bag. Once people learn how to use it, it can be used to wrap almost anything, including two bottles of wine, a whole watermelon, or books.

The word *furoshiki* comes from the Japanese word *furo,* which means "bath."

In the 14th century, it was first used as a wrapping cloth for carrying clothes to the public baths. Then, merchants began using it as a wrapping cloth for their products. It also became a perfect tool for advertisements. During this time, varieties of beautifully designed *furoshiki* appeared throughout Japan.

Now, it is a popular souvenir for overseas tourists.

How to tie *furoshiki*: *ma-musubi* knot (the fundamental knot)

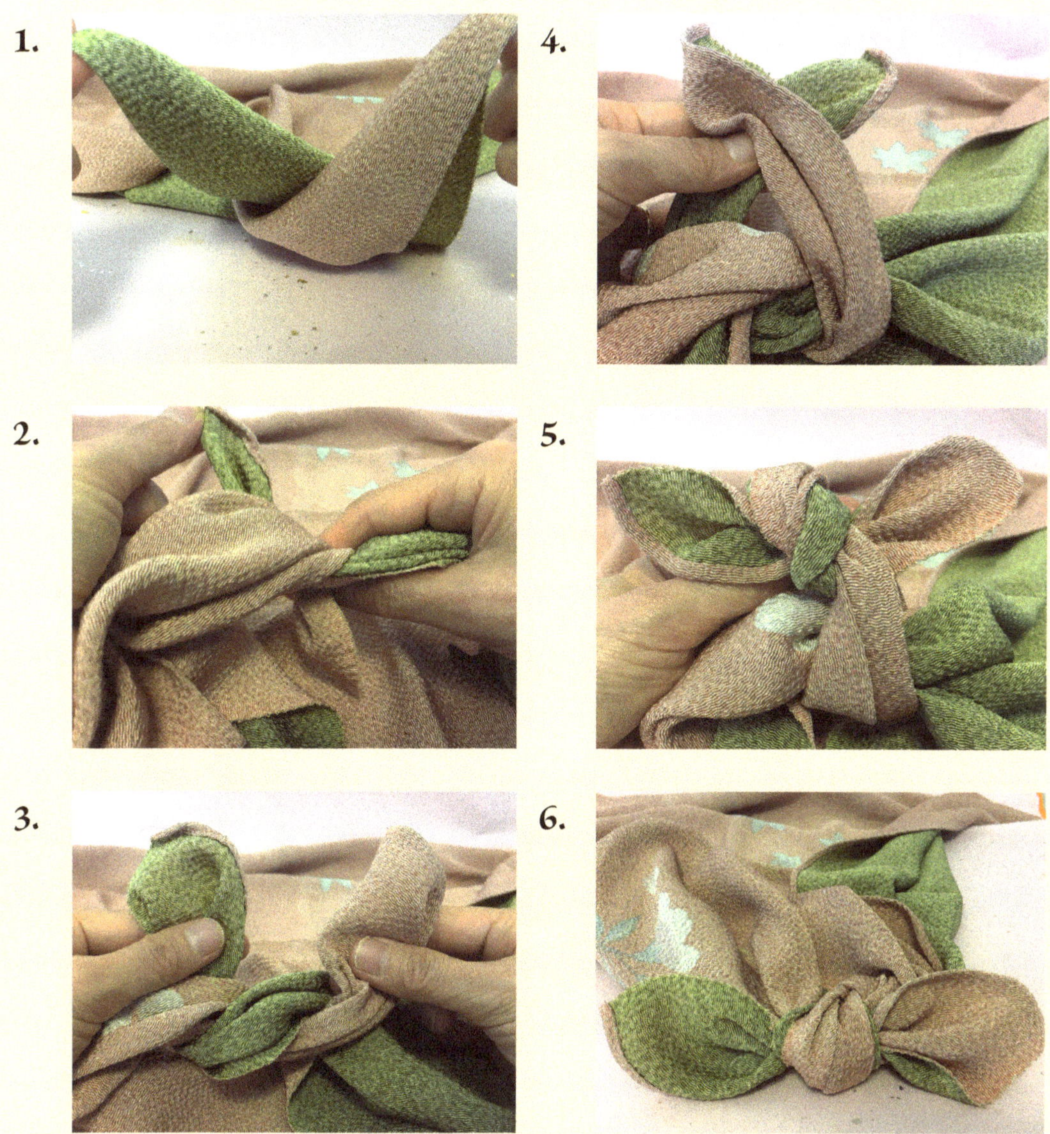

How to wrap two bottles

1.
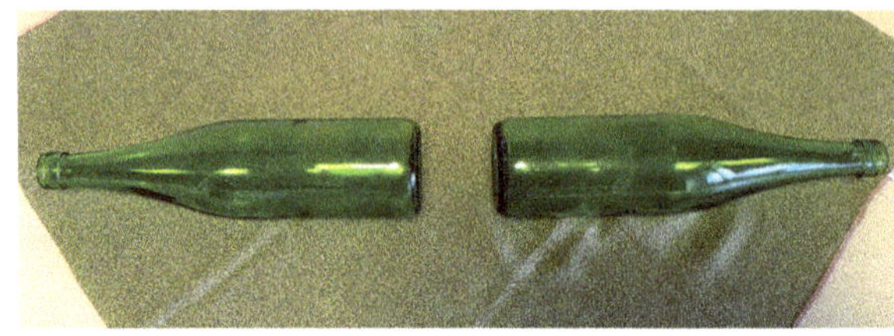

2.
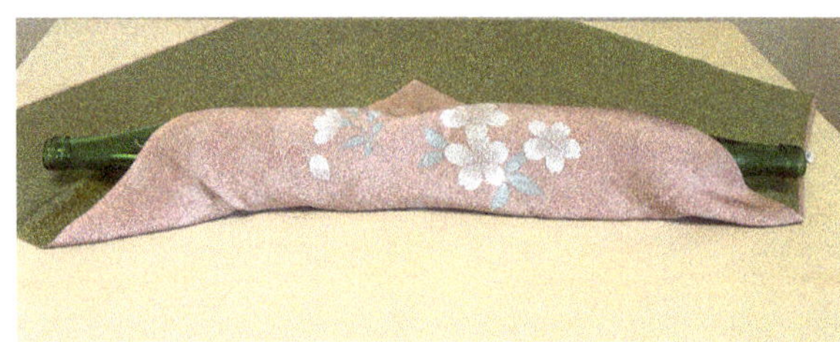

3.
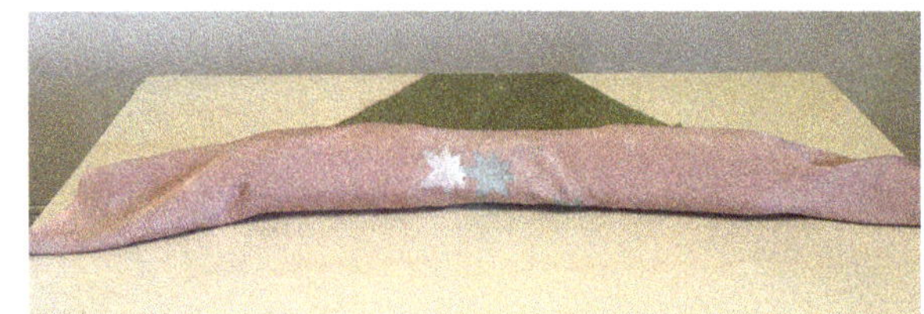

4.
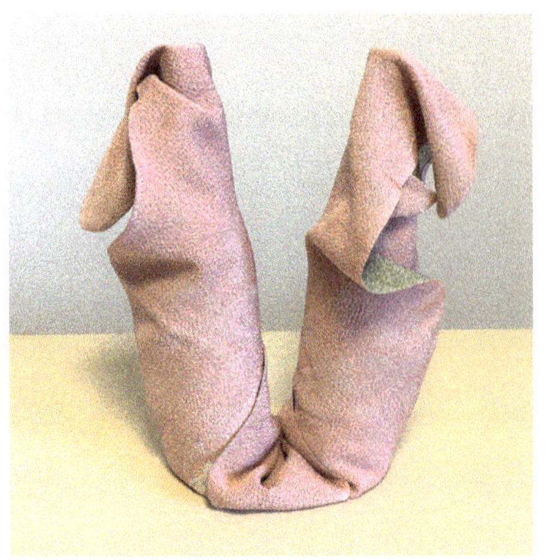

5.
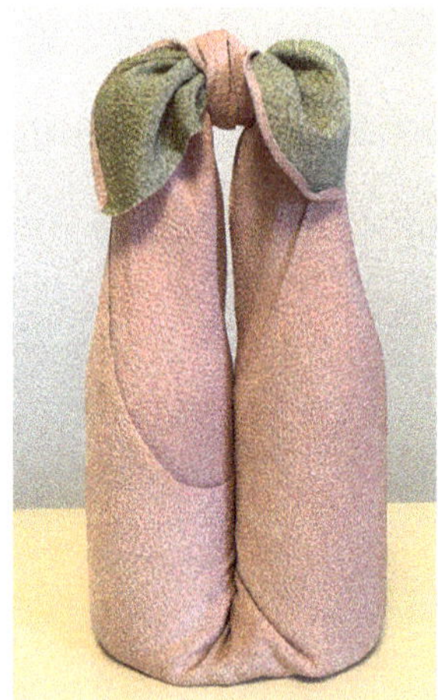

How to wrap a bottle in a kimono style

1.

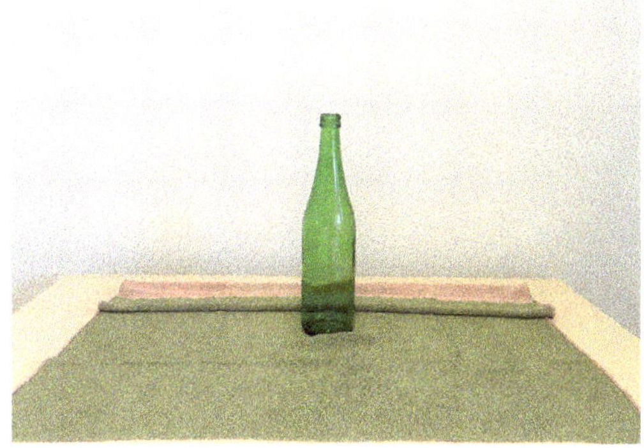

2.

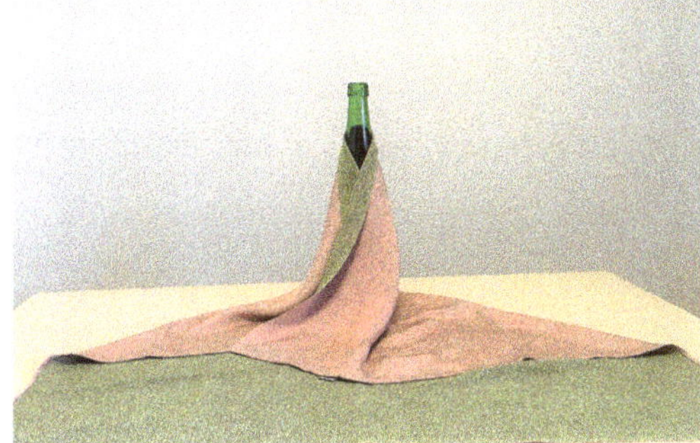

3.

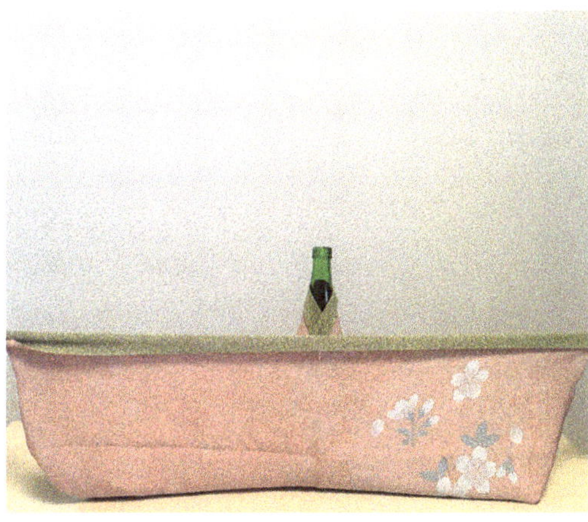

4.

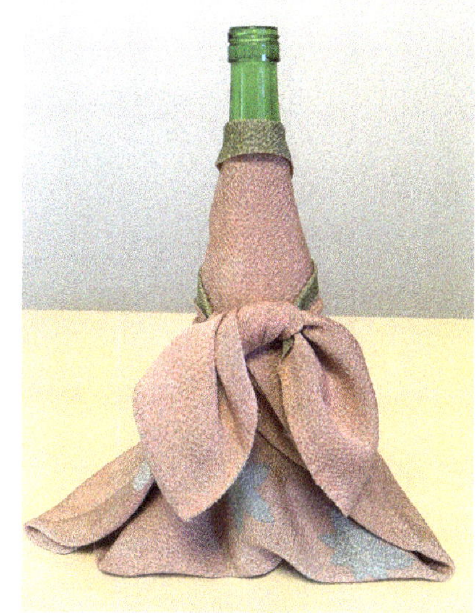

back side

5.

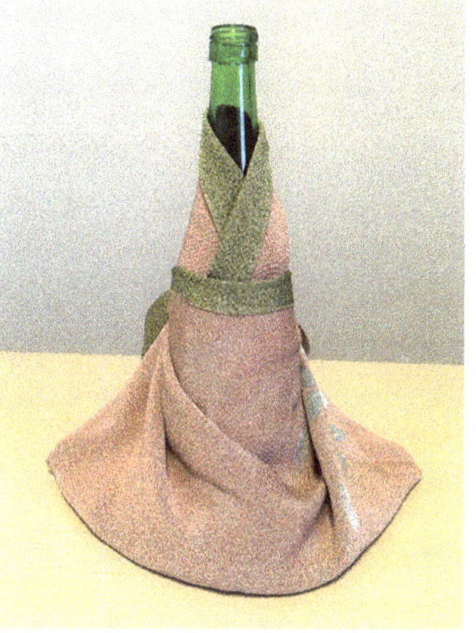

front side

How to wrap a plastic bottle

1.

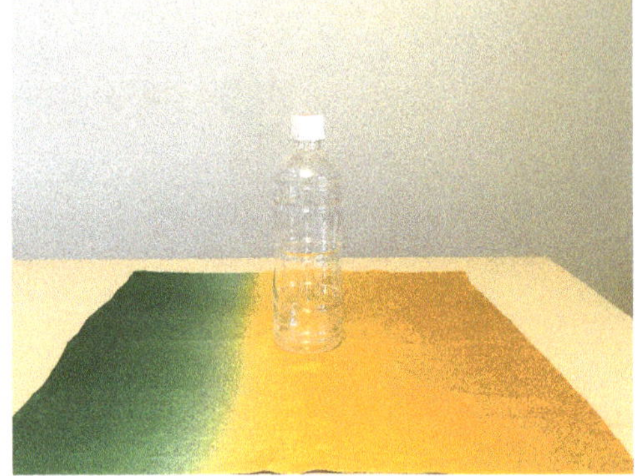

4.

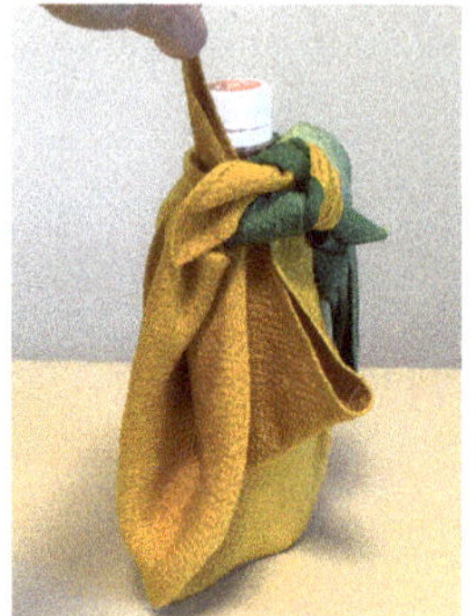 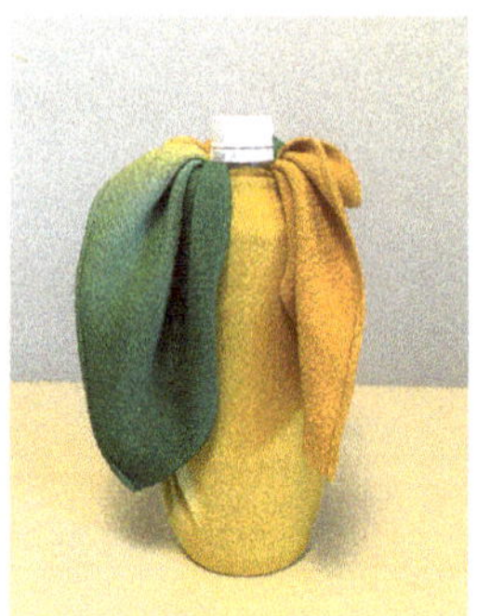

2.

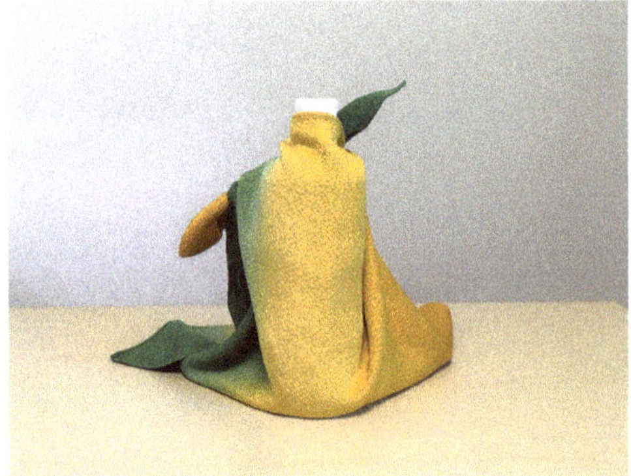

3.

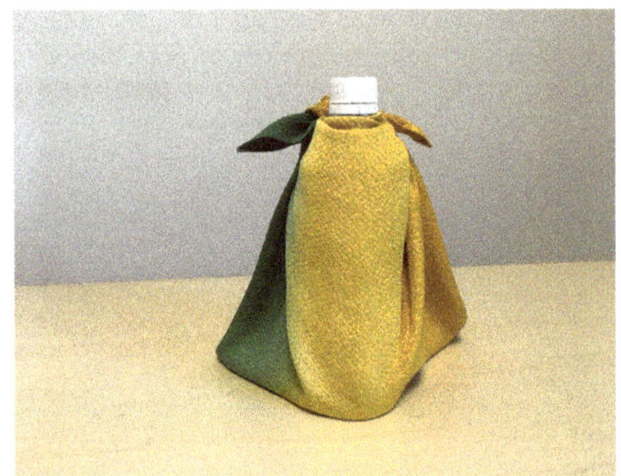

5.

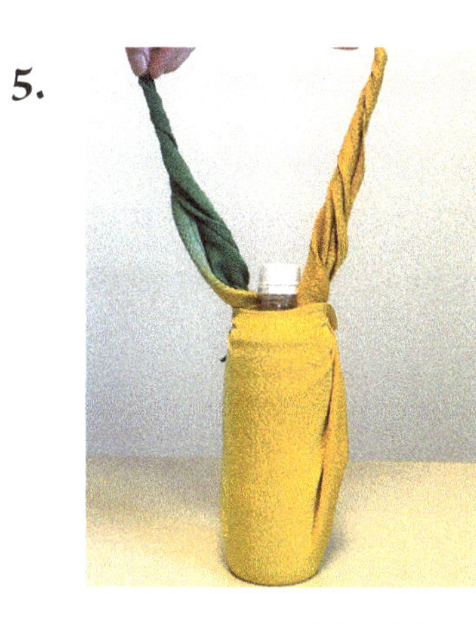

6.

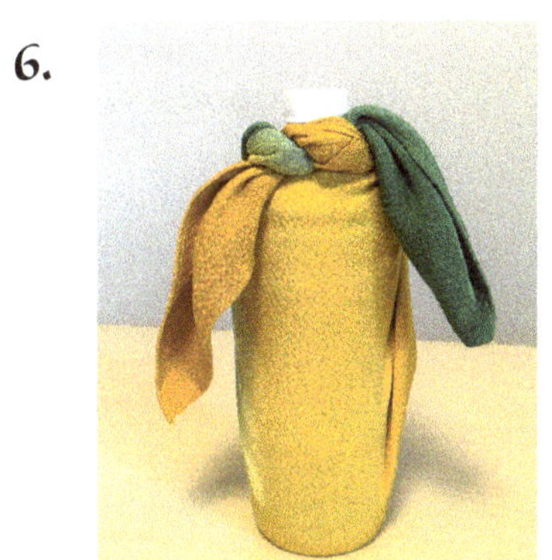

7.

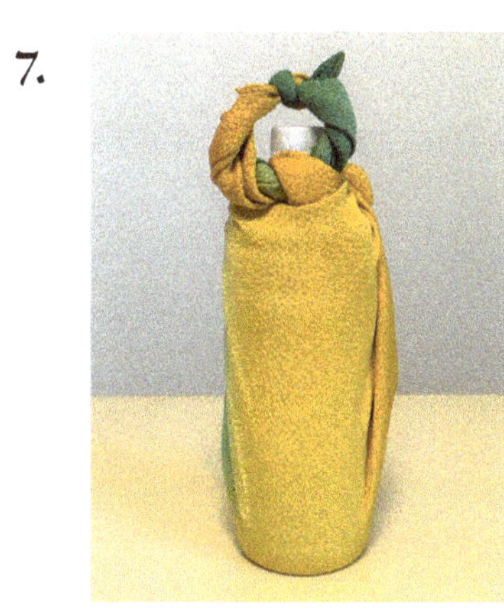

8.

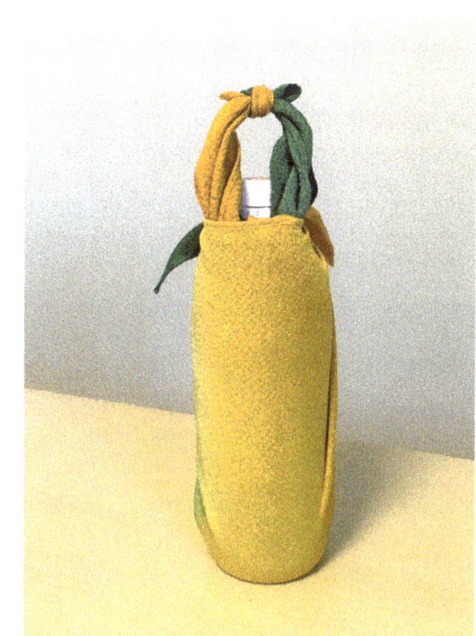

back side

9.

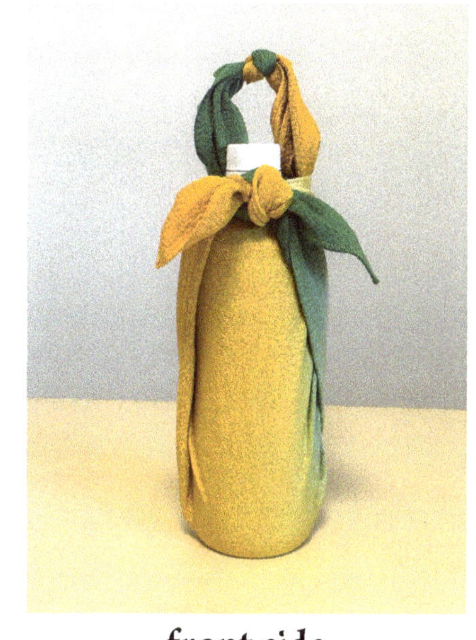

front side

Kaishi: Japanese paper napkins

Kaishi is a multipurpose Japanese paper that is carried in a kimono. It is used as a paper plate or a paper napkin during the Japanese tea ceremony. It is the perfect accessory for expressing sophisticated manners while wearing a kimono.

Unlike typical paper napkins prepared by Western restaurants, it is considered elegant to use one's own *kaishi* while dining at classy Japanese restaurants. Japanese restaurants often do not prepare paper napkins, so *kaishi* can be used instead.

It can also be used for a variety of other purposes, such as a paper towel and memo paper.

Kaishi

How to fold kaishi

Auspicious occasions

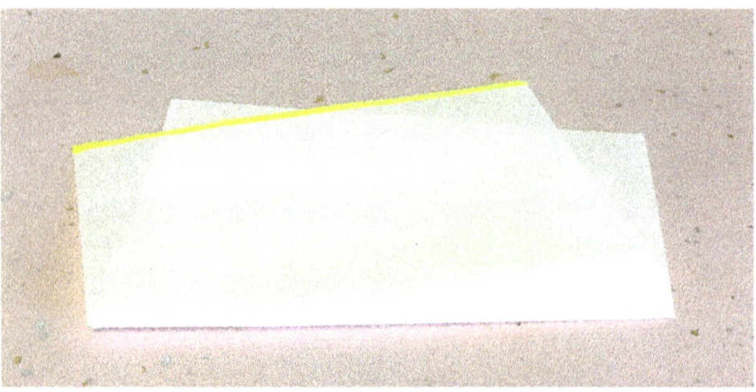

Mourning, memorial

CHAPTER 7

History of the Japanese Kimono

History of the Japanese Kimono

The Heian Period: From the 8th to the 12th century

In those days, *junihitoe*, or twelve-layered kimono, was invented for ruling class court nobles.

This layered kimono was suitable for the four Japanese seasons.

Today, only imperial-family members wear it at special ceremonies.

The colors of this twelve-layered kimono are based on the seasonal colors of nature.

The standards for the arrangement of the layers were inspired by the unique sense for beauty of the Japanese people. This unique sense has been handed down from generation to generation.

The Kamakura and the Muromachi Periods: From the 12th to the 16th century

Around the end of the 12th century, Japanese society dramatically changed. Warriors were called *samurai*. They were initially guards of the imperial authority. Later *samurai* came to have power. The *samurai* leader was called *shogun*. The first *shogun* opened the new government in the 12th century. Japanese kimonos also greatly changed—for example, in the previous period, kimonos for aristocrats were very intricate and complicated. *Kosode*, originally an under-layer for aristocrats' kimonos, began being featured in those days.

The Azuchi-Momoyama Period: The latter part of the 16th century (exactly 1573–1603)

Japan proactively imported beautifully woven cloths from China.[1] "Regime changes not only transformed governments but also brought about new fashion trends and modes of presenting oneself to society."[2]

The cloths were also used for the costumes for traditional Japanese stage dramas, called *Noh*. Kimonos began to show a variety of designs.

The Edo Period: From the 17th to the 19th century (exactly 1603–1867)

From the 17th to the 19th century, Japan had a centralized government.

In the Edo period, foreign exchange was limited. This means that Japan did not widely communicate with Western countries.

---

1 *Kimono Fashioning Identities*, the catalogue for the special exhibition at Tokyo National Museum shown 14th, April through 7th June, 2020, published by *The Asahi Shinbun TV* Asahi Corporation, 2020, p. 371-399
2 *Ibid.*

Because of this isolationist policy, Japanese culture developed uniquely. The Japanese art of the Kimono was one example of a handicraft utilizing Japanese weaving and dyeing techniques. *Yuzen* dyeing is a good example. These free-form pictorial designs sparked a fashion revolution.

It is said that the current kimono style was established in the Edo period.

Kabuki also started as a popular stage drama at the time. Ordinary people began imitating the fashionable kimono styles of the actors. In the middle of the 19th century, the Edo period ended. It meant that the last *shogun's* government ended.

The Meiji Period: From the 19th century to the beginning of the 20th century

Japan began to widely open to Western countries again. At this time, many Japanese people experienced Western clothes for the first time. Upper-class people began enjoying Western garments along with Japanese kimonos and accessories. The current method of tying *obi* sashes was established.

The Taisho Period: Beginning of the 20th century

At the beginning of the 20th century, Japan was becoming more modernized. People enjoyed Western fashion and new styles of kimonos. Some of the new techniques were invented in those days. *Meisen* kimonos are representative of one of them. (P110)

Dyeing and weaving techniques were developed for the production of artificial materials and use of machines. Thanks to this development, many new designs of kimonos appeared.

During this period, Japanese fashion dramatically changed.

The Showa Period: During the 20th century

The number of people wearing Western clothes increased during the 20th century.

However, traditional kimonos were handed down, especially for formal occasions. Some modern kimonos made by artists became popular as well.

After the Heisei Period to the Reiwa period: After the 20th century

Standards of dress for traditional Japanese kimonos have been passed down to the 21st century, although there have been slight changes over time.

Additionally, new styles of modern kimonos are being created every day. For example, one of the most famous contemporary kimono designers, Rumi Rock, produces beautiful kimonos using traditional Japanese techniques.

Rumi Rock kimonos were displayed in an exhibition in London in 2020. It attracted a huge number of people from all over the world. (P108)

CHAPTER 8

Beautiful Postures and Elegant Behavior While Wearing a Kimono

1) Beautiful postures for taking pictures

While Western clothes tend to emphasize the lines of the body, kimonos emphasize the original square forms of the cloth. Therefore, posing with straight body lines is considered most elegant for those wearing a kimono.

When posing for pictures while wearing a kimono, the model should have a straight posture and turn the body slightly to the side. It is essential to show the sleeves of the kimono and the *obi* sash, making a single, cohesive image. One hand is held slightly lower, and one foot is slightly back.

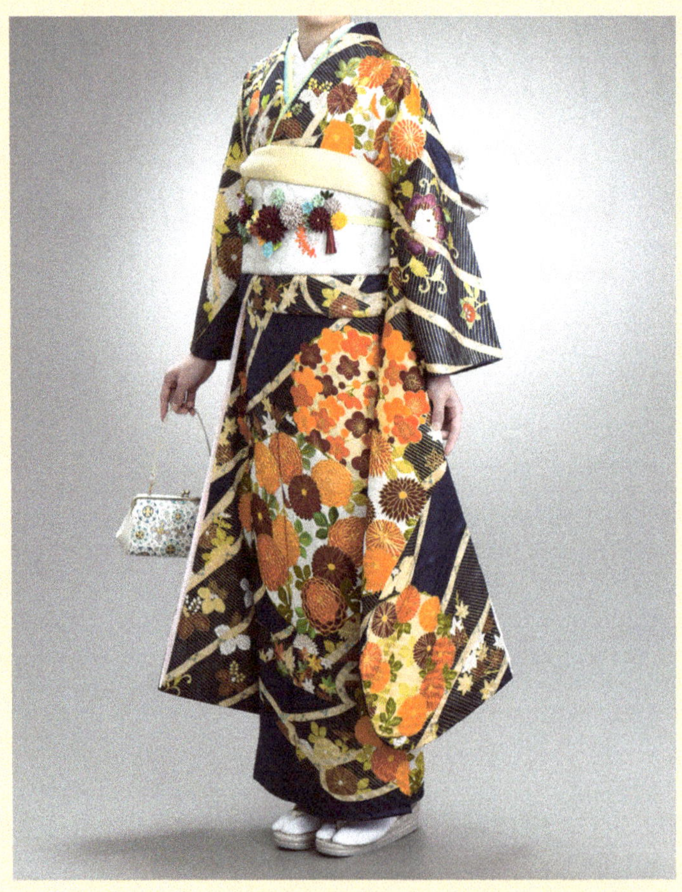

2) Elegant behavior while wearing a kimono

How to walk

While wearing a kimono, it is considered elegant to walk with toes turned inward and knees touching. Short steps are also considered to be graceful.

When inside a Japanese style room, it is important to avoid stepping on the edges of *tatami* mats. *Tatami* is a Japanese-style floor mat made of rush.

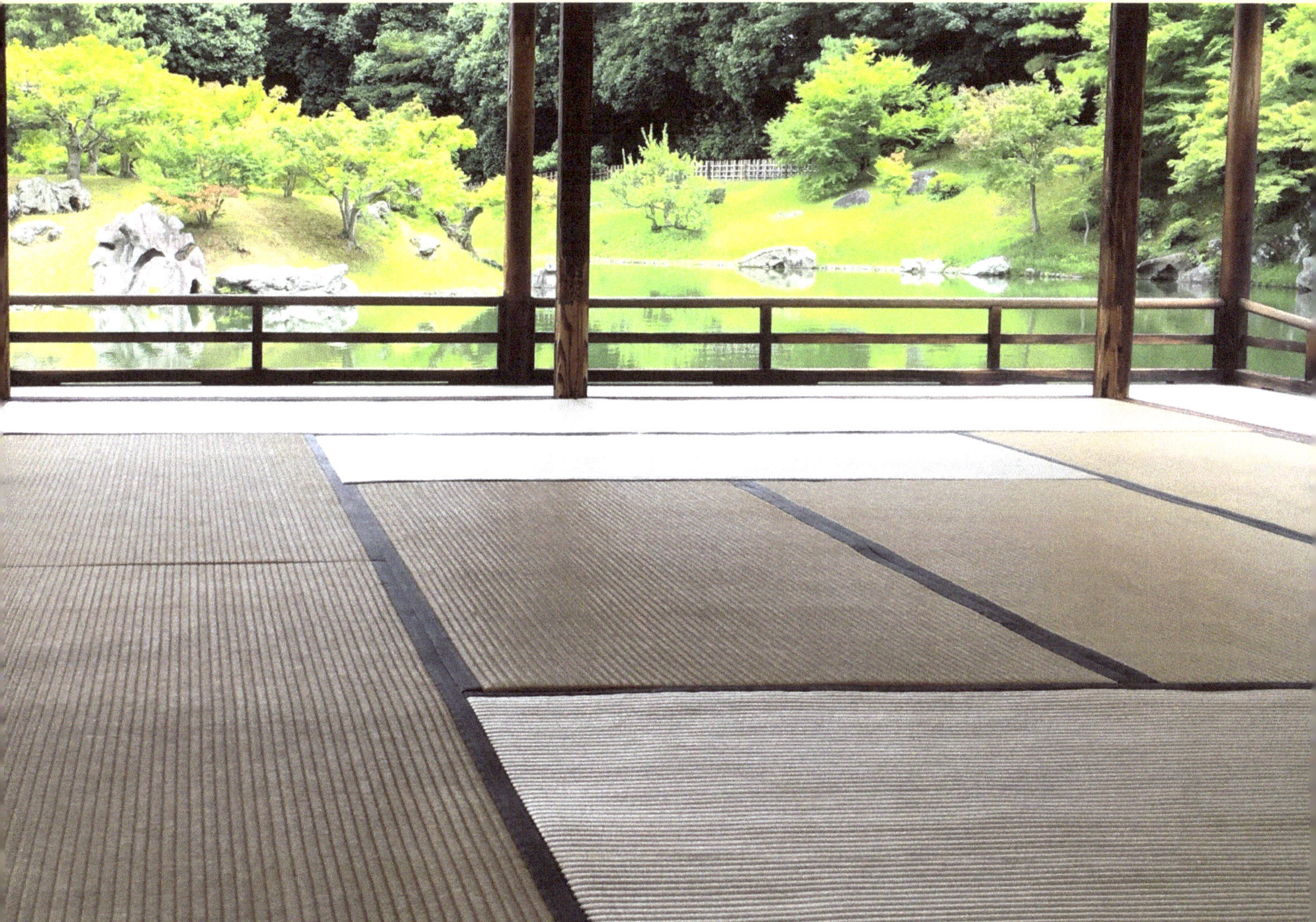

How to bow

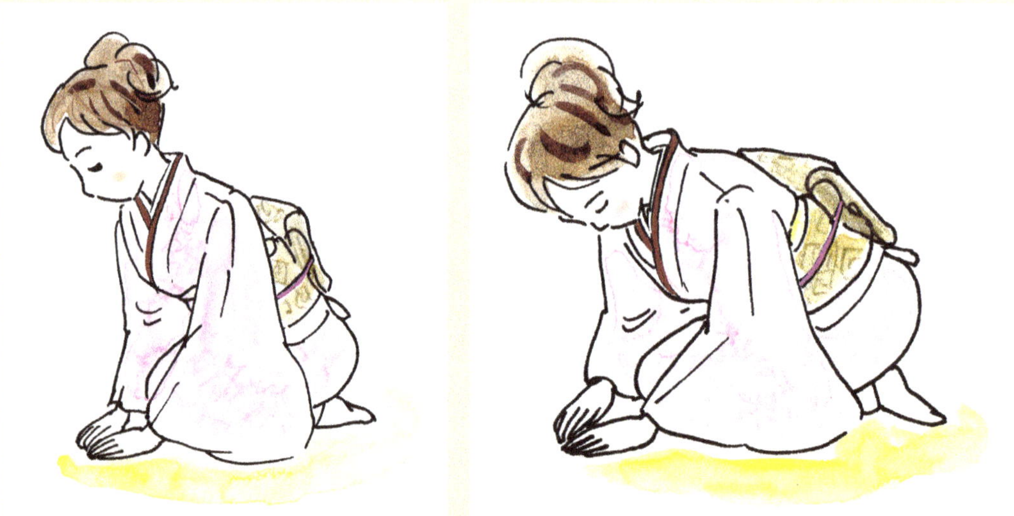

How to be seated on a Japanese cushion

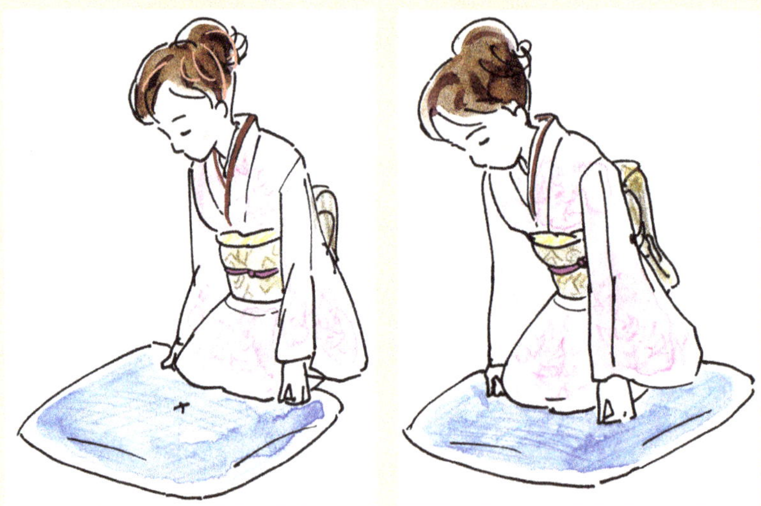

How to walk up and down steps

When walking up and down steps, hold up a lower part of the kimono to raise the hemline, and face the body slightly sideways. In this way, people can climb steps gracefully without stepping on the kimono's hemline.

How to get into a car

When getting into a car, first sit on the seat with feet outside of the car. Then, hold up the front of the skirt of the kimono, and slide both feet inside the car at the same time. When getting out of a car, complete these steps in reverse.

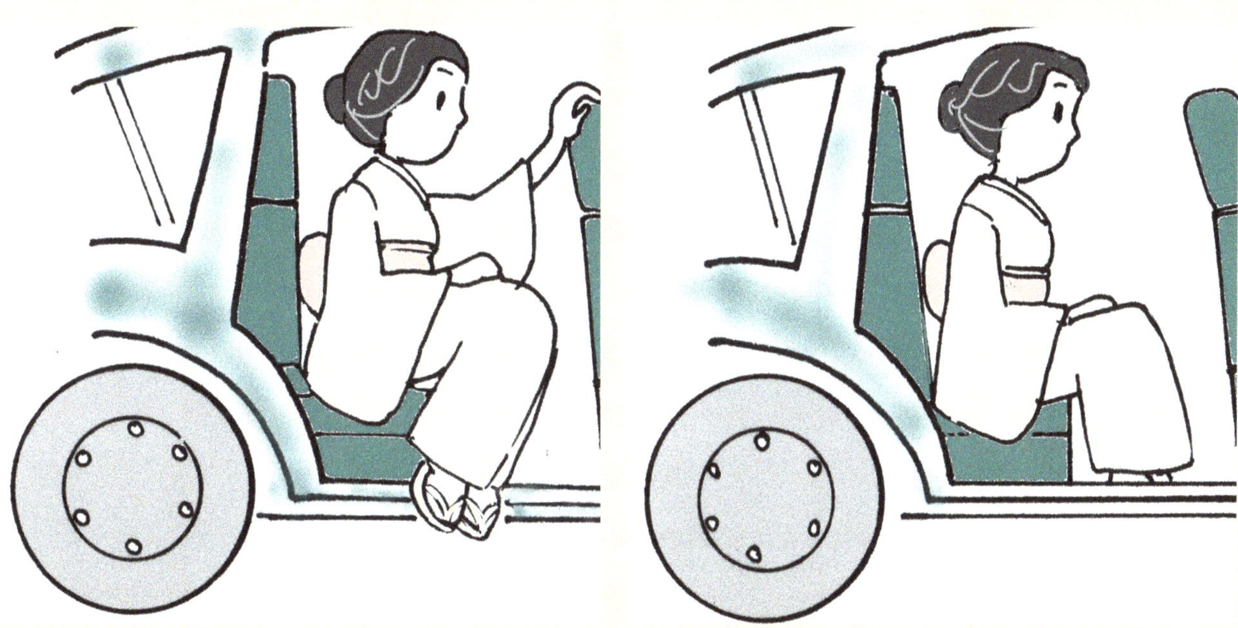

CHAPTER 9

Special Shops
and Information

1) Rumi Rock: A top contemporary-kimono designer

https://www.rumirock.com/

Rumi Rock started as a *yukata* brand. It was created by RUMIX DESIGN STUDIO in 2005.

Rumi Rock's design incorporates the spirituality of the Edo period (P98) street fashion, and elements from fairy tales.

High-quality Japanese fabrics are dyed with contemporary designs using traditional techniques.

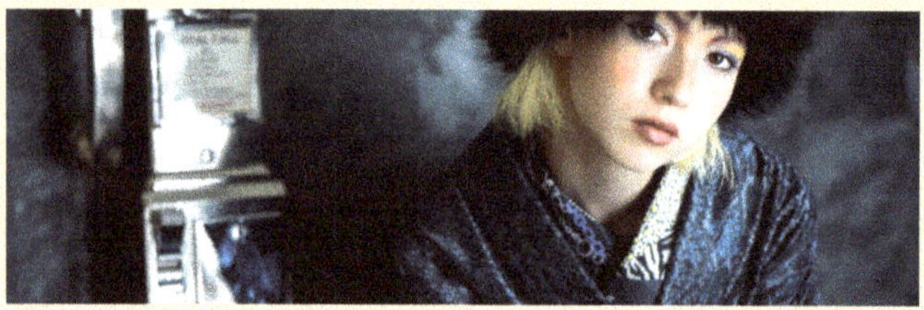

Rumi Rock kimonos were exhibited in the Victoria and Albert Museum in 2020.

This exhibition attracted a huge number of people from all over the world.

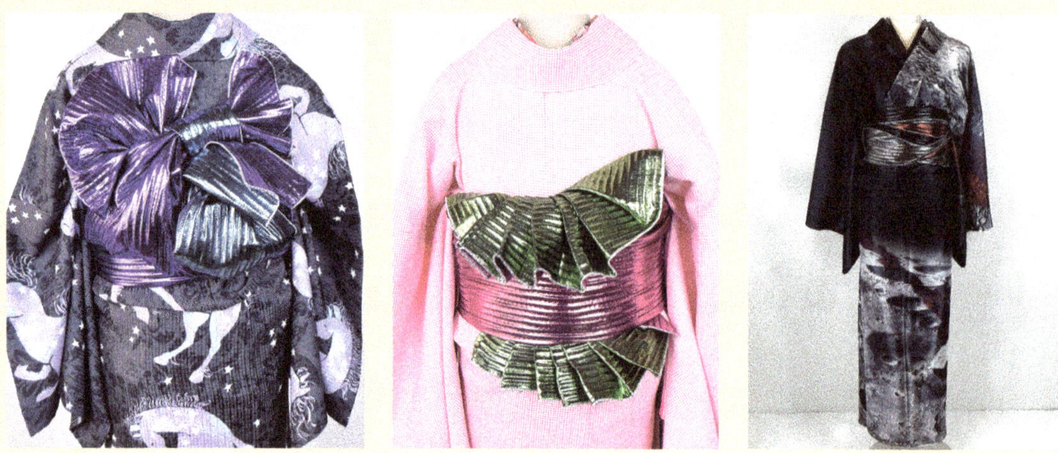

Instagram http://shop.rumirock.com/

Contact (English available) info@rumirock.com

2) Futabaen: A traditional cloth-dyeing experience venue

Name: Futabaen

Access: Seibu Shinjuku Line Nakai Station (SS04),
Subway Toeioedo Line Nakai Station (E32)

Address: 2–3-6 Kamiochiai, Shinjuku, Tokyo

Open: 11:00 a.m. to 5:00 p.m.

Closed: Monday

URL: http://www.futaba-en.jp/index.html

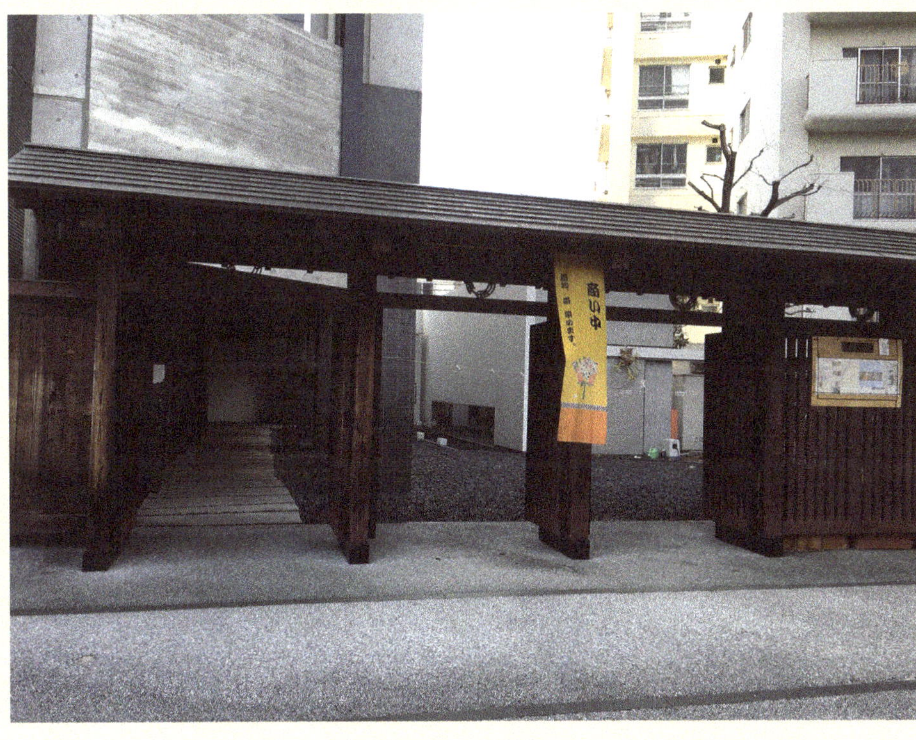

3) Yamazaki: A shop where you can make your own traditional kimono

For those who would like to make their own, custom-made kimono, a kimono shop named "Yamazaki" is recommended. This shop is a traditional Japanese kimono shop, with more than fifty years' history.

The owner, Mr. Yamazaki, can communicate with customers in English. When people order a tailor-made kimono, clear communication with each other is essential.

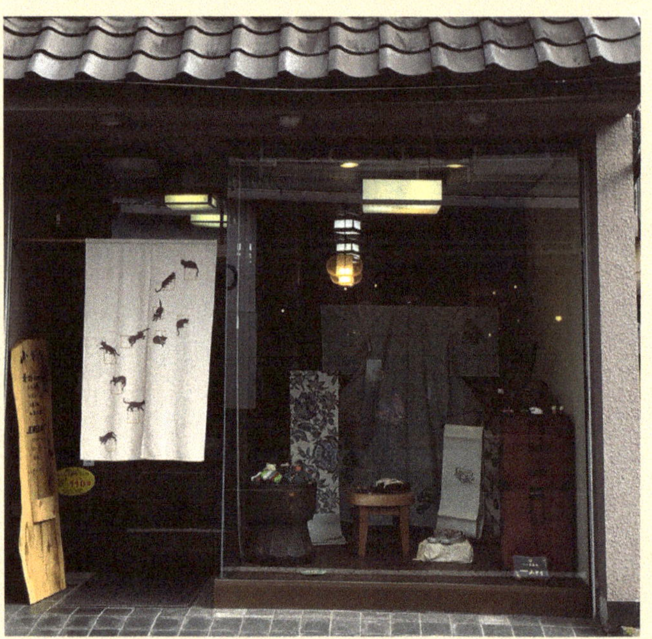

Mr. Yamazaki provides the high-quality materials and techniques necessary to make the best kimono for each customer.

Name: Yamazaki
Address: 3–2-9 Yanaka, Taito-ku, Tokyo
Access: 10 minutes from JR Line Nippori station
Open: 11:00 a.m. to 7:00 p.m.
Closed: Wednesday

4) Meisen+: Information on coordination of *Meisen* kimonos

Meisen is one of the genres of the traditional daily kimono from the early 20th century .

This collection shows how to coordinate them to go well with today's lifestyles.

Facebook: Meisen+
https://www.facebook.com/113691193362896/posts/119140559484626/

CHAPTER 10

How to Put on Yukata

How to put on a woman's *yukata*

1. Put the *yukata* on like a robe. You will adjust for your size later. **The important point is that the right side is first and that the left side is over the right side.**

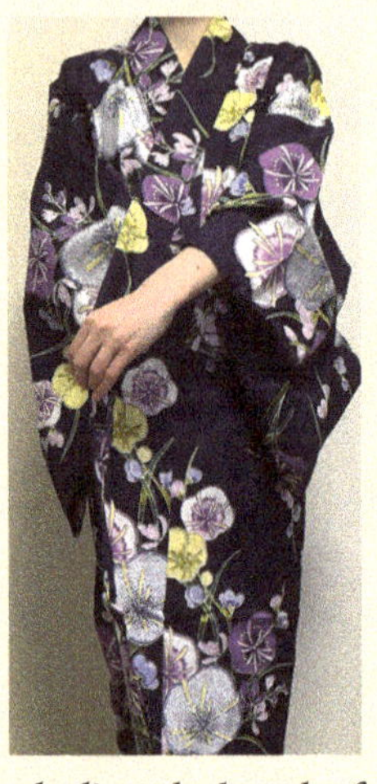

2. Make sure the vertical seam on the back is at the center of your body.

3. Open the *yukata* with both hands, and adjust the length of the hemline by sliding the material up until it is straight and just covering your ankles. (no picture)

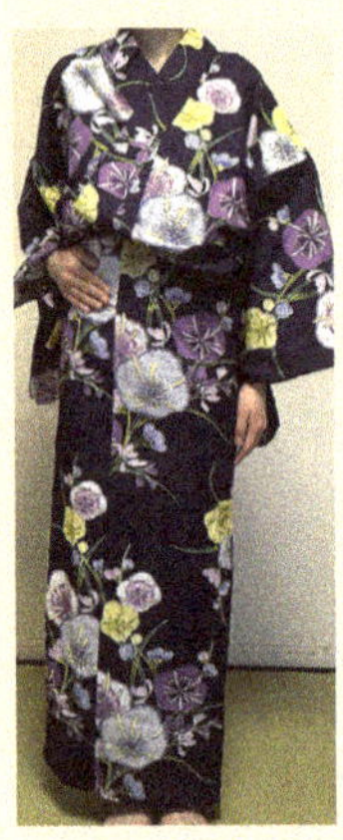
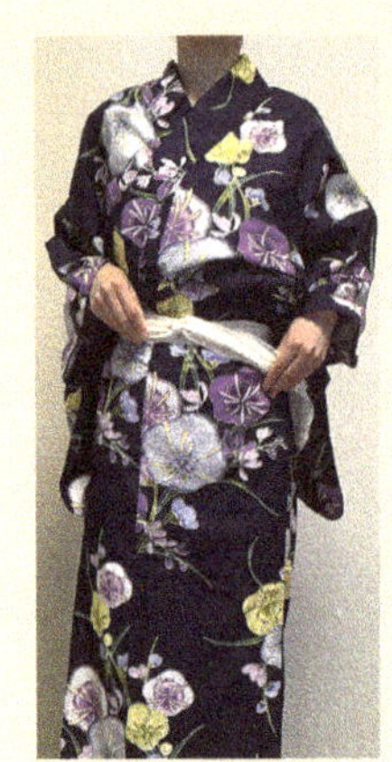
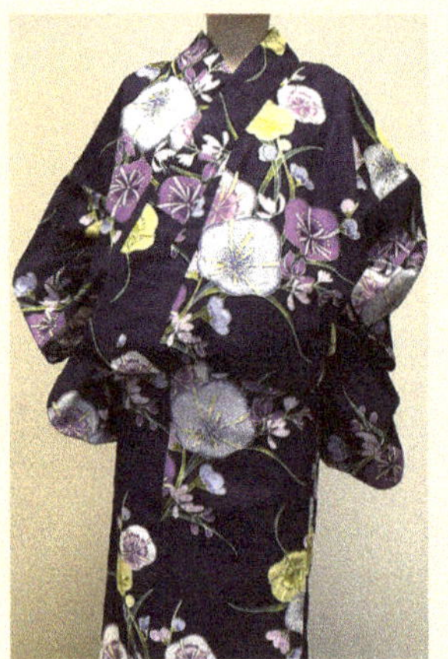
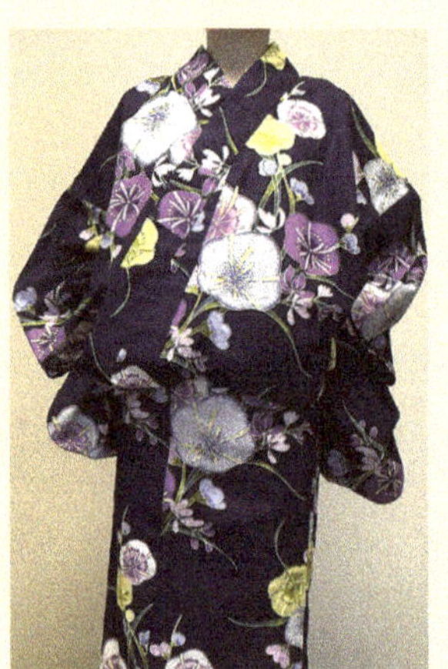

4. Fold the right side across your body again. Then fold the left side over the top.

5. Tie a thin cotton string around your waist to ensure that the hemline stays in place.

6. Smooth down any excess material in the front or back over the cotton string.

7. Fasten the *yukata* with an inner belt just under your chest to hold the fabric in place.

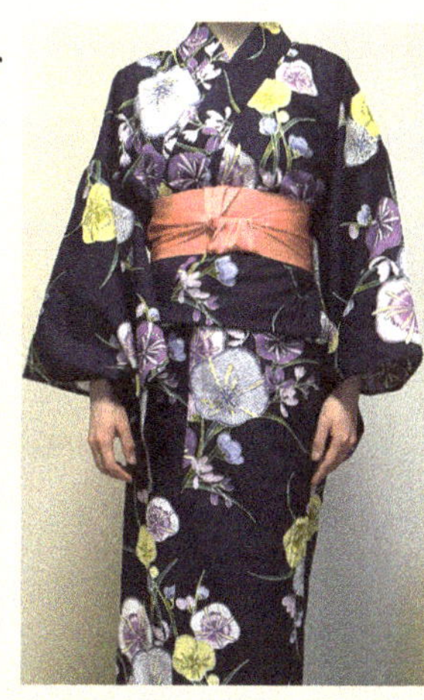

How to tie an *obi* sash

1. Hold the end of the *obi* sash with your right hand. Wrap the *obi* sash twice around your body.

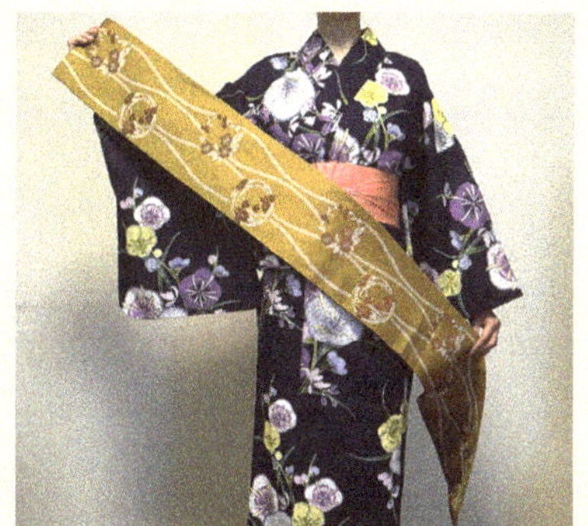

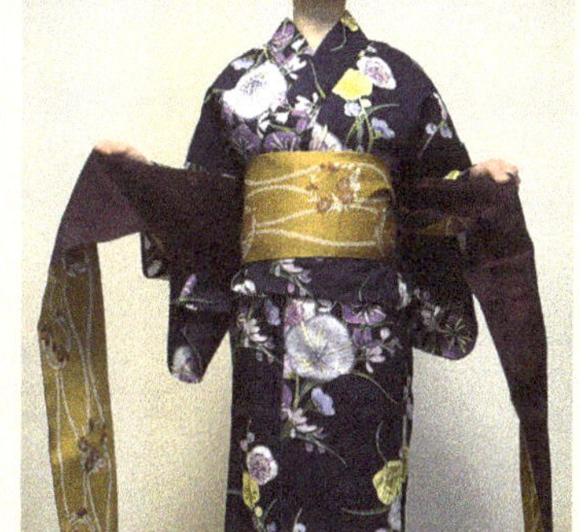

2. When both ends are about the same length, make a knot at the front.

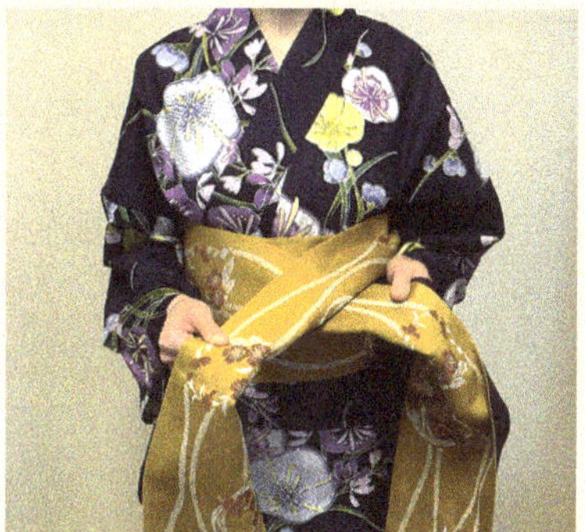

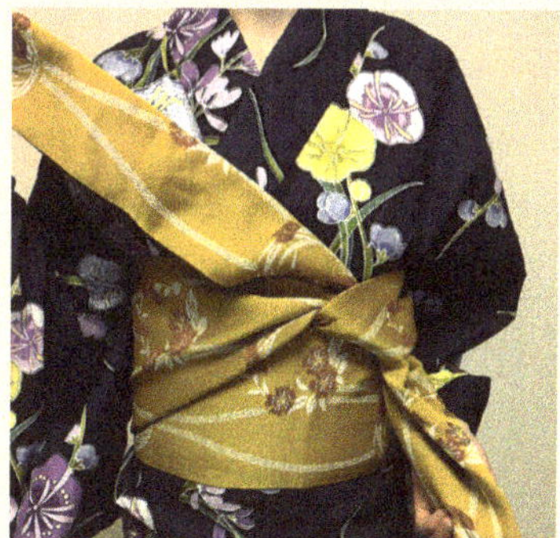

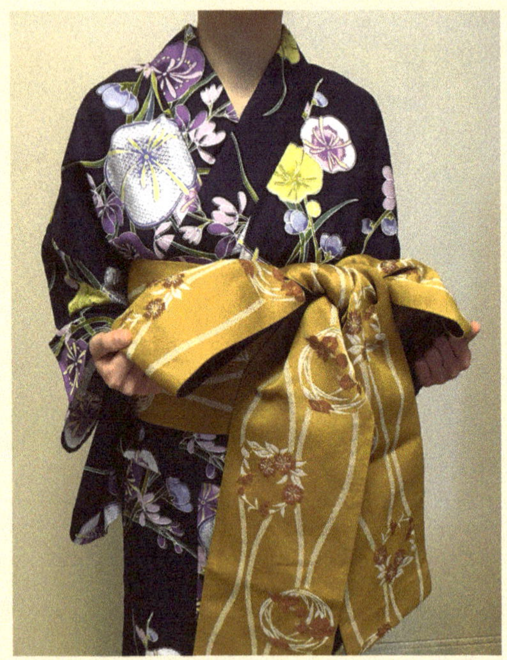

3. Tie the *obi* sash into a bow at the front.

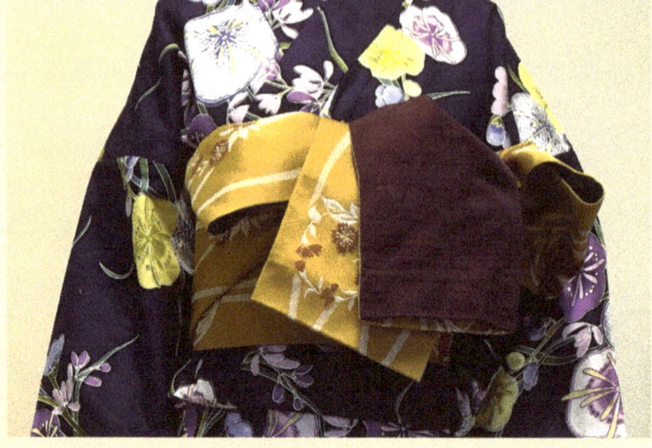

4. Both ends of the sash can be used as decorative trims.

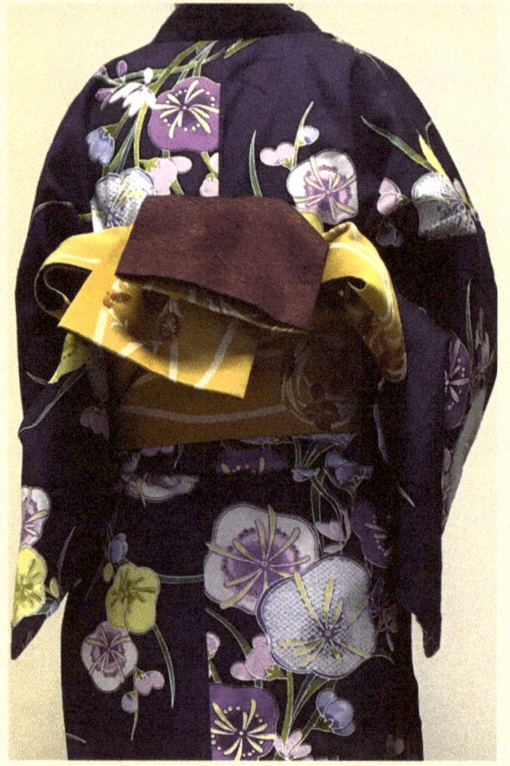

5. Turn the *obi* sash clockwise 180 degrees
   so that the bow is in the back.

How to put on a man's *yukata*

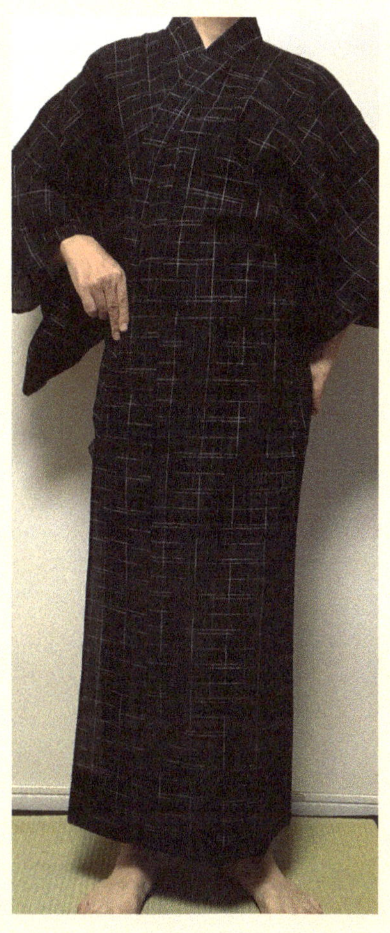

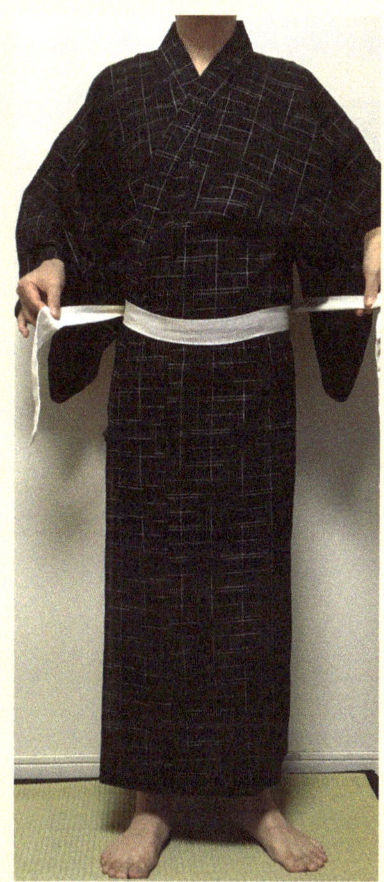

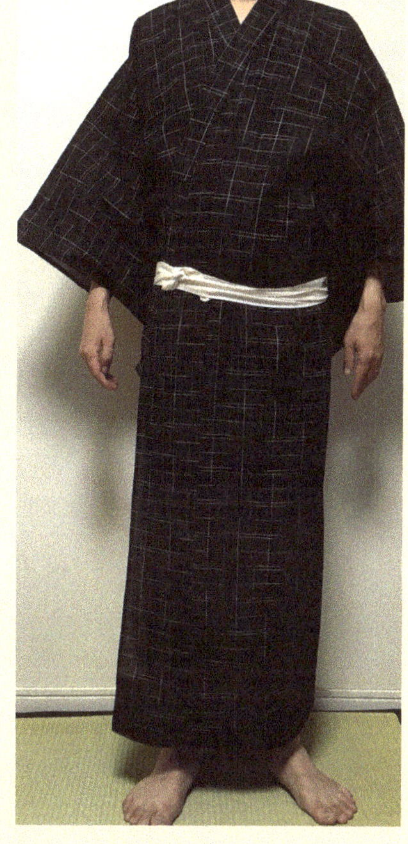

1. Choose the proper size. Fold the right side across your body. Then, fold the left side over the top. **The important point is that the right side is first and that the left side is over the right side.**

2. Tie a thin cotton string around your waist. The position of the cotton string should be slightly higher at the back.

How to tie an *obi* sash

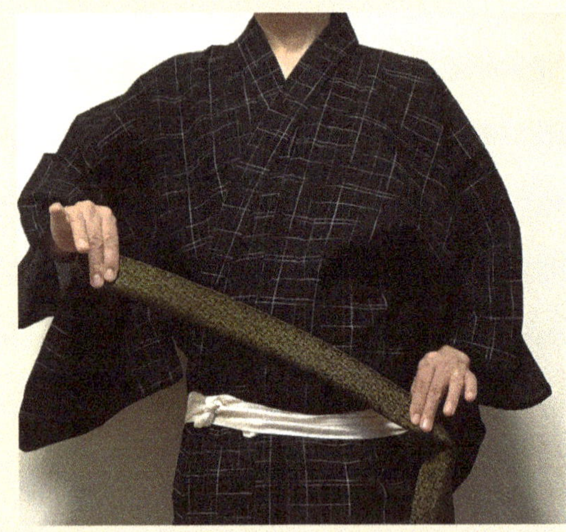

1. Pick up one end of the *obi* sash and fold it in half to about 30 centimeters from the end.

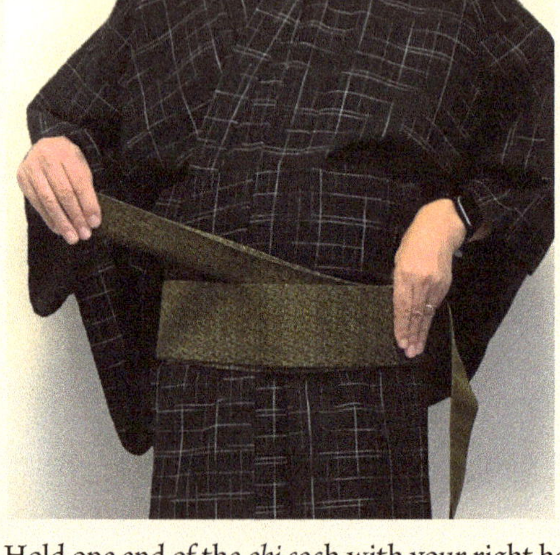

2. Hold one end of the *obi* sash with your right hand. Wrap the *obi* sash once or twice around your body.

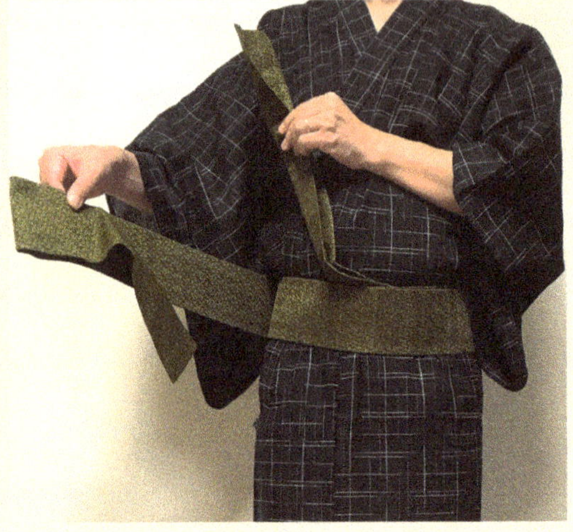

3. If the *obi* sash is too long, the outer end can be folded inward to match the length of the other end.

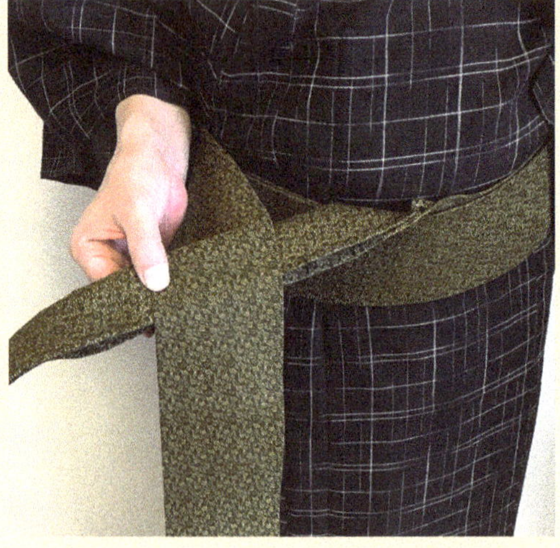

4. When both ends are about the same length, make a knot at the front. The outer end should be in the upper position when tied.

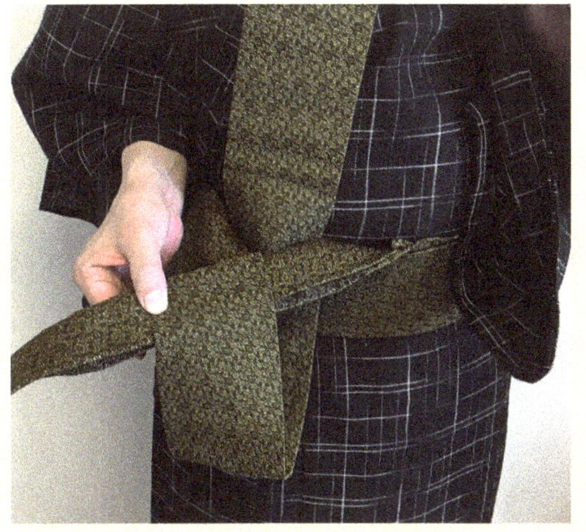

5. Pull both ends vertically.

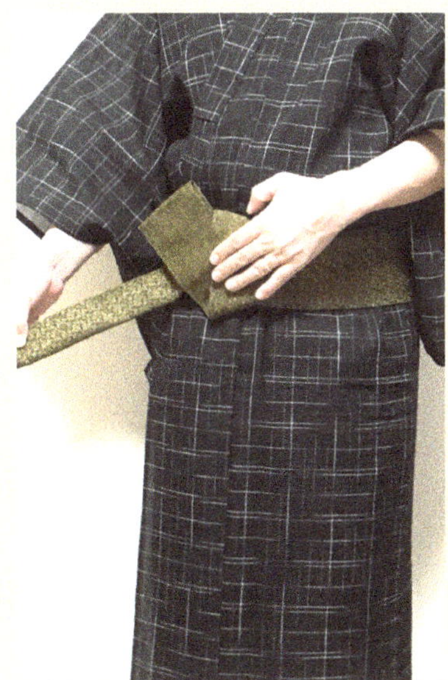

6. Fold the upper end in half. Insert the lower end into the folded upper end.

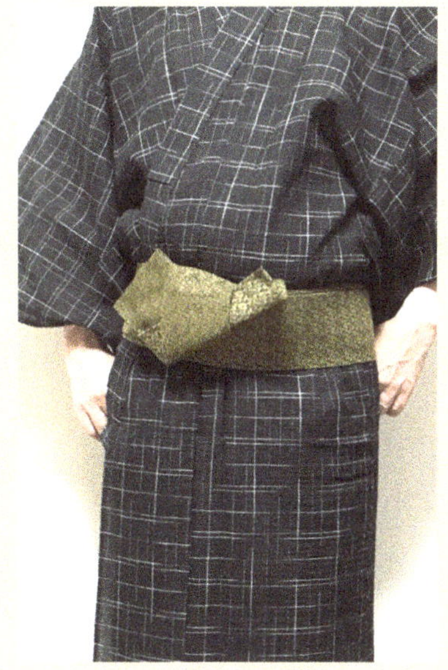

7. Pull both ends tightly and shape it.

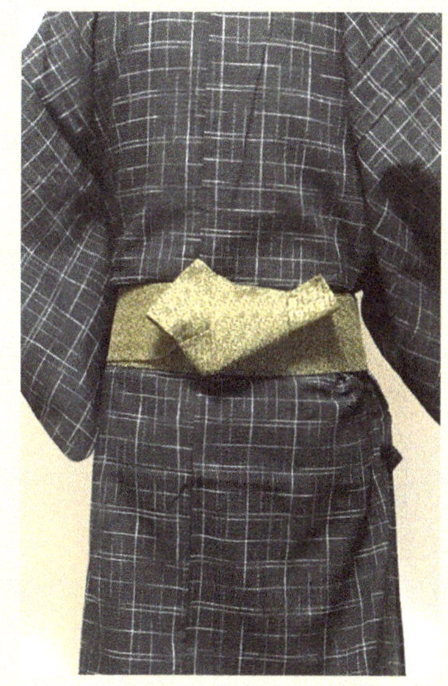

8. Turn the belt clockwise 180 degrees to the back.

I hope you enjoyed this book. Would you do me a favor?

Like all authors, I rely on online reviews to encourage future sales. Your opinion is invaluable. Would you take a few moments now to share your assessment of my book on Amazon or any other book review website you prefer? Your opinion will help the book marketplace become more transparent and useful to all.

Thank you very much!

www.ingramcontent.com/pod-product-compliance
Lightning Source LLC
LaVergne TN
LVHW070952180726
843512LV00017B/1224